Governance of Higher Education

SIX PRIORITY PROBLEMS

A Report and Recommendations by
The Carnegie Commission on Higher Education
APRIL 1973

MCGRAW-HILL BOOK COMPANY

New York   St. Louis   San Francisco   Düsseldorf

London   Sydney   Toronto   Mexico   Panama

Johannesburg   Kuala Lumpur   Montreal

New Delhi   Rio de Janeiro   Singapore

This report is issued by the Carnegie Commission on
Higher Education, with headquarters at
1947 Center Street, Berkeley, California 94704.
The views and conclusions expressed in this report
are solely those of the members of the Carnegie Commission
on Higher Education and do not necessarily reflect the
views or opinions of the Carnegie Corporation of New York,
The Carnegie Foundation for the Advancement of Teaching,
or their trustees, officers, directors, or employees.

Library of Congress Cataloging in Publication Data
Carnegie Commision on Higher Education.
Governance of higher education.
1. Universities and colleges—United States—
Administration. I. Title.
LB2341.C164   378.1'01   73-4774
ISBN 0-07-010062-4

Additional copies of this report may be ordered from McGraw-Hill
Book Company, Hightstown, New Jersey 08520.
The price is $4.50 a copy.

Government is not an exact science.

LOUIS D. BRANDEIS
Opinion in Truax v. Corrigan

My experience in government is that when things are noncontroversial, beautifully coordinated, it must be that there is not much going on.

JOHN F. KENNEDY
Quoted in Bill Adler, The Kennedy Wit

If we ask ourselves on what causes and conditions good government in all its senses, from the humblest to the most exalted, depends, we find that the principal of them, the one which transcends all others, is the qualities of the human beings composing the society over which the government is exercised.

JOHN STUART MILL
Representative Government

Contents

Foreword

This report on governance is primarily concerned with six issues that are of particular current urgency: (1) adequate provision for institutional independence, (2) the role of the board of trustees and of the president, (3) collective bargaining by faculty members, (4) rules and practices governing tenure, (5) student influence on the campus, and (6) the handling of emergencies. It also offers some general observations about campus governance and makes suggestions that go beyond the confines of the six issues above.

We define governance as the structures and the processes of decision making. We thus distinguish it from administration or management.

Other Commission reports have also been concerned with aspects of governance:

- *The Capitol and the Campus* favored (1) less direct control over public institutions by governors, (2) coordinating councils that confined themselves to planning and coordination, and did not attempt to assume the power of administration over individual institutions, (3) appointment of trustees of public institutions after appropriate impartial screening and subject to legislative confirmation, and (4) limitation of public authorities to general policy formation.

- *Dissent and Disruption* (1) proposed a "Bill of Rights and Responsibilities" to govern conduct of all members of the campus community, (2) favored consultative machinery available in emergencies, and (3) supported the need for independent judicial bodies.

- *The More Effective Use of Resources* counseled against line-item control of budgets by public authorities.

- *Reform on Campus* (1) favored student participation in curricular formation and in evaluation of the teaching performance of faculty members, and (2) supported internal decentralization into "cluster" and "theme" colleges, and into other partially self-governing internal units.

Governance in academic communities has become very complex. Yet few careful studies of it have been made until very recent times, and few balanced commentaries on the subject are available. Most of the commentaries about it are written from a point of view partisan to one group or another—whether public authority, or campus administration, or faculty, or students—or partisan to one single theory of governance. The issues of governance are also very controversial. In the midst of this complexity and this controversy, we offer our best current judgment. We do not attempt a careful description of actual governmental practices, which are very diverse, ranging from dominant faculty influence in some of the leading private research universities to dominant board and presidential influence in many of the public community colleges.

Campuses have been called "ungovernable anarchies." We see them instead as institutions marked by conflicts and confusions over purposes and processes, by the mobility of major participants—as faculty members but particularly students move in and out—and by great sensitivity to the tensions of a society undergoing rapid change. Marked by these and other characteristics that make governance difficult, campuses are, we believe, both governable and worth governing well.

One special feature of this report is information about student and faculty attitudes on aspects of governance. These data are drawn from Carnegie Commission surveys of student and faculty opinion carried out under the direction of Martin Trow, University of California, Berkeley, with the particular assistance of Joseph Zelan.

A second special feature is Appendix C, which sets forth recommendations on the six issues from a series of other reports on this subject.

Several studies undertaken for the Commission have been helpful in formulating this report, including *Recent Alumni and Higher Education: A Survey of College Graduates*, by Joe L. Spaeth and Andrew M. Greeley (McGraw-Hill, 1970); *The Multicampus University*, by Eugene C. Lee and Frank M. Bowen (McGraw-Hill, 1971); *Any Person, Any Study*, by Eric Ashby (McGraw-Hill, 1971); *American Higher Education*, by Joseph Ben-David (McGraw-Hill, 1971); *The University as an Organization*, by James A. Perkins, ed. (McGraw-Hill, 1973); *Academic Transformation:*

Seventeen Institutions under Pressure, by David Riesman and Verne A. Stadtman, eds. (McGraw-Hill, 1973); *The Organization of Ambiguity: The American College President*, by Michael D. Cohen and James D. March (forthcoming); *The Academic System in American Society*, by Alain Touraine (forthcoming); "Creeping Unionism and the Faculty Labor Market," by Joseph W. Garbarino (in *Higher Education and the Labor Market*, Margaret S. Gordon, ed., forthcoming); *Change in University Organization Power: 1964–1971*, by Edward Gross and Paul V. Grambsch (forthcoming); and *Some Dilemmas in Higher Education Today*, by Michio Nagai (forthcoming).

The Commission has consulted with three conference groups about special problems of governance. The members of these groups were: Albert Bowker, Chancellor, University of California at Berkeley; William Boyd, President, Central Michigan University; Kevin Collins, Student Body President, University of California at Davis; Alice Cook, Ombudsman, Cornell University; David E. Feller, Professor of Law, University of California at Berkeley; Joseph W. Garbarino, Director, Institute of Business and Economic Research, and Professor of Business Administration, University of California at Berkeley; Donald Hartsook, Ombudsman, University of California at Los Angeles; Sanford H. Kadish, Professor of Law, University of California at Berkeley; Harold Kittner, Ombudsman, Kent State University; George Leitmann, former Ombudsman, University of California at Berkeley; Jack Little, Ombudsman, University of California at Irvine; Jerry Mahoney, Ombudsman, California State University at San Diego; Ken Maley, Student Body President, California State University at San Francisco; William McHugh, Special Counsel for Employment Relations, State University of New York; Morton Orenstein, Supervisory Attorney, National Labor Relations Board, Western Regional Office; Richard Peairs, Regional Director, American Association of University Professors, Western Regional Office; Ralph Poblano, former Ombudsman, California State University at San Jose; Howard Ray Rowland, Director of Information Services, St. Cloud State College; James Rust, former Ombudsman, Michigan State University; Larry Seidman, Student Body President, University of California at Berkeley; Lloyd Ulman, Director, Institute of Industrial Relations, University of California at Berkeley; Stephen Williamson, Research Coordinator for Student Body President's Council, University of California at Berkeley; and Donald Wollett, Professor of Law, University of California at Davis.

The Commission expresses its appreciation to members of its staff who assisted with this report and particularly to Dr. Lois Swirsky Gold for her preparation of Appendix A and Appendix C and for her general assistance.

Governance of
Higher Education

1. Major Themes

1 The governance of higher education in the United States is currently more subject to challenge than it has been in most earlier historical periods. It has been subject, particularly over the past decade, to a number of internal and external attacks and collisions. This development reflects the pressures of conflict and change now affecting academic life, because both conflict and change make the processes of decision making more important to those who participate in, or are substantially affected by, higher education. Central issues have been raised. Basic principles are at stake.

2 Viewed from the perspective of the past century, however, the governance system of higher education in the United States has been adequate to the tasks of accommodating vast increases in student members and of providing a concurrent improvement in academic quality. The magnitude of these accomplishments attests to the general sufficiency of the governmental processes that have existed in the past, but they are, nevertheless, now under attack because of changed circumstances.

3 External authorities are exercising more and more authority over higher education, and institutional independence has been declining. The greatest shift of power in recent years has taken place not inside the campus, but in the transfer of authority from the campus to outside agencies.

4 Some students continue to seek more participation through voting rights on committees and through formal consultation, although only a few really want control over academic life. This effort, rising and falling in intensity, is likely to continue into the indefinite future.

5 Most faculty members are cautiously willing to concede more consultation to students but are generally opposed to granting voting rights to students in areas primarily of faculty concern. They, like the students, often want more influence vis-à-vis administrators, trustees, and external authorities. For the first time they are seriously considering collective bargaining in a substantial number of institutions.

6 Many aspects of higher education relate to campus-level governance, such as the size and internal organization of campuses, and the number and compatibility of the functions performed. We set forth a list of major aspects with which each institution should be concerned as it reviews the environment within which governance occurs, and we indicate directions for action.

7 We see these particular areas for the further evolution of academic governance:

- More effective approaches to the preservation of reasonable institutional independence.

- The need for independent and devoted boards of trustees to enhance the external independence and the internal equilibrium of the campus, and for presidents with sufficient power and influence to give leadership in a period of ferment and change.

- Careful analysis, particularly by faculty members, of the professional implications of the resort to formal collective bargaining, and of the comparative values of alternative patterns of governance.

- Better adaptation of tenure practices to the current realities of academic life. By 1985, we are likely to have 80 percent of full-time faculty members with tenure, if current tendencies continue, and over 90 percent with tenure in 1990.

- Increased opportunities for students to participate in governance in areas of their interest and competence.

- Better advance preparation for the handling of emergency situations.

8 Governance may now be entering a new period marked by continuing conflict rather than by the informal consensus that characterized it in the recent past. If so, it will need to undergo substantial restructuring to meet the strains of conflict. We hope, however, that, to the extent possible, a new consensus may be achieved. For this to occur, some restructuring will also be necessary, but the resulting processes will be animated by a more tolerant spirit.

9 Governance is a means and not an end. It should be devised and adjusted not for its own sake but for the sake of the welfare of the academic enterprise.

2. The Governance of Higher Education in the American Context

The governance of institutions of higher education around the world is marked by great variety from nation to nation, ranging from direct and detailed control by the central government (as in the Soviet Union) to the laissez faire of private profit-making enterprises (as found in some institutions in the Philippines) with many constellations of arrangements in between. Within each nation, however, there tends to be a standard pattern of governance. A general commonality of governing arrangements has occurred more within than among nations.

The governance of higher education in the United States has features that distinguish it from systems elsewhere. One of its unique features is the great diversity of forms between and among institutions—more so than in most other nations where greater internal uniformity applies. Our system, with all its comparatively great internal variations, however, has been especially characterized by these general features:

1 Absence of centralized control by the national government—essential authority has rested with state governments and with boards of trustees.

2 Concurrent existence of strong public and private segments.

3 Trustee responsibility—basic responsibility to provide for governance of individual institutions has been in the hands of lay boards in both public and private institutions.

4 Presidential authority—the president has had substantial executive authority delegated by the lay board.

5 Departmental authority—within the faculty, the department has been the key unit of academic organization over most of the past century.

In contrast with these arrangements, in a number of other

5

countries (as in most of Western Europe and in Latin America) (1) the central government has had more control, (2) the private sector has not been as strong, (3) a council of deans or of senior faculty members has performed many of the functions of the lay board in the United States, (4) the role of the president has been carried out more largely on a ceremonial level by a rector either elected for a short term by the senior faculty or appointed by the central government, and (5) faculty authority has rested with the "chair" professors, who are arranged into broad "faculty" groupings. But governance in many countries has been changing rapidly and the forms it takes are, of course, diverse. The American system, however, has had, and continues to have, more authority vested in instrumentalities intermediate between the central government and the senior faculty members—the board of trustees and the presidency—than has been the case in most or even all other nations; and it also has allowed more participation by junior faculty members than in many other nations. The campuswide administration has been a comparatively strong point of power.

The origins of the American system lie in:

- The separation of church and state, which helped to lead to a separation of higher education and the state, since many of the early colleges were started by religious groups
- A democratic and pluralistic system with many centers of power
- A federal system of national, state, and local governments
- The Protestant concept of lay control over the clergy, which helped lead to lay control also over the faculty members who in the early days were often also clergymen
- A capitalistic system with private ownership boards and strong executives
- The rise of the authority of the discipline that particularly accompanied the expansion of science and specialization
- The expectation of the protection of individual freedom of speech for faculty members as for others

and in other aspects of American religious, political, economic, and social life.

The governmental structures of higher education have followed patterns generally consistent with the patterns of the larger American society. They have constituted a generally compatible subsystem within the larger social system, although a subsystem with a substantial degree of independence. This subsystem has changed just as has the larger social system. The power of the church has eroded; campus control over individual student behavior has declined; more activity has been channelled over time through public instrumentalities and less through private; the national government has come to exert more influence. The major transformations in the governance of higher education over the centuries since the founding of Harvard in 1636 have been these, and more or less in this order:

1 The gradual diminution over a long period of time in church influence with the rise of public institutions and the secularization of church schools

2 The increase in the authority of the college president, particularly after the Civil War, as institutions became larger, more complex, and more dynamic, and as administration became more professional

3 The extension of greater academic freedom to faculty members and of greater faculty control over academic affairs especially since World War I, and particularly as faculty members took on more of the status of independent scientists and experts

4 The decline of *in loco parentis* control over students, a decline that accelerated after the Civil War and again after World War II

5 The increase in direct public influence and authority generally, and in federal influence and authority in particular, especially since World War II

6 The rise of multicampus systems of higher education, which now enroll nearly one-half of all students, and of coordinating councils and superboards

7 The decline in the role of the single-campus board as all these other changes have occurred

The overall system of governance of higher education in the United States, as it has evolved, has been generally noteworthy for these results in the past, and they continue largely into the present:

• The system has operated substantially, but not completely, outside of partisan politics both because of internal resistance and of external forbearance.

- Public support has been substantial and persistent.

- Great diversity among individual institutions has marked the overall system of higher education.

- The system has been comparatively dynamic in its ability to change and to adapt to growth, to new fields of endeavor, and to new groups of students.

- It has been comparatively responsive to public interests, as in its service activities and as in its extension of equality of opportunity to increasing numbers and diverse groups of people.

- Individual campuses and multicampus systems have had substantial administrative and academic independence.

- It has provided particularly high-quality research and Ph.D. training, and much other professional and occupational training of good quality.

Great and inconsistent pressures in recent years, however, have been placed on this historically effective overall structure. Not only are these pressures greater than ever before in American history, but they tend to be more at cross-purposes with one another:

- In the span of a few decades, higher education has moved from a system designed for a relatively small and more-or-less socially elite group to one providing broad access; and it is now moving toward universal access. There are not only many more students, but the students are also more diverse in their interests and in their levels of academic preparation and competence.

- In the 1970s, growth in enrollments is slowing down from the rate of the past century, and will temporarily cease entirely in the 1980s. In the absence of growth, change will be much more difficult to effect; expanding fields, for example, will not be add-ons, but replacements. The determination of appropriate proportions of tenured faculty members in the total faculty and the development of provisions for early retirement are other examples of intensified issues as growth slows, beyond those of a more dynamic period.

- The financial situation has become more difficult, and there is, as a consequence, more controversy over the internal use of resources. Faculty salaries and working conditions are improving less rapidly than they did in the 1960s—when they improve at all—and this leads to more faculty organization and more aggressive faculty action to protect its position.

- Campuses have become larger and more complex; there are more levels of decision making within the campus and above the campus. Decisions often take more time and are farther removed from the operating level. Loyalty to the institution is less likely to develop as size increases and complexity multiplies. Also, the strengthening of professional relationships has been drawing attachments away from the campus.

- Students have become more active in the general affairs of the campus and of society. Their methods of recent years have included direct confrontation—sometimes illegal—with authority. This has caused strains on campus and divisiveness in relations with society.

- Faculty members are more in conflict about the purposes of academic life. There is a growing split between those who seek objectivity and those who pursue ideological commitment, and between those who wish to preserve standards and those who favor adjusting standards to the situation of the individual student. Some faculty members (about 5 percent) declare themselves to be "left" in political orientation (see Appendix A, Tables A-1 through A-5), and political orientation is strongly associated with some contrasting approaches to academic governance, as we shall note below. Five percent is a small percentage, but its members can initiate large actions in a crisis—when most others are confused and/or uninvolved. A political "dissensus" has developed on campus.

- The public interest in higher education is more intense. Higher education takes more of the resources of society.

- More families have a direct interest in how the campus conducts itself. It is more involved in local and national political affairs. It is more the source of controversial lifestyles. And fewer people are willing to leave it to its own devices. As a consequence, public authority is more aggressively exercised over higher education.

- A general reduction in the acceptance of authority has marked many aspects of American society in recent years; so also on the campus. Respect for laws and regulations has declined among sizable numbers of persons both on and off campus.

- There has been a similar reduction in the sense of loyalty to institutions; on campus, for example, more faculty members are "cosmopolitans" and fewer are members of the "home guard" than in times past, and more administrators are "professionals" without deep institutional attachments.

- There is more emphasis upon participation as the sine qua non to legitimize decisions and less on assigned responsibility and accountability; and more stress upon the informal and ephemeral group than upon the formal and permanent agency.

- Many people have become more concerned with their individual rights and less concerned with the welfare of institutions.

These are among the many pressures now at work on the structures and processes of governance. Their individual intensity causes problems, but these problems are heightened in their gravity by the contradictory nature of the pressures. Public interest works in the direction of public control; but student and faculty activism works in the direction of local control by the direct participants. Faculty and student activist sentiment is in favor of more self-governance; but the reduction in a sense of consensus among faculty members and students makes such self-governance more difficult. The cessation of growth calls for more flexibility in making readjustments in past patterns of operation; but faculty collective bargaining organization may mean more rigidity and more attachment to the status quo ante. Financial stringency often requires more centralized control of decisions affecting expenditures; but central control is also more suspect. These cross-pressures are illustrative of the general problem of the swirling crosscurrents affecting governance.

The two most unusual features of the system of governance in the United States are the ones now under the most pressure: the intermediary institutions of (1) the board of trustees and (2) the presidency. The board of trustees historically has held the "trust"—the guardianship of the long-run welfare of the institution. Under current circumstances, it must also be more of a "buffer" as campus and community are more at odds, and more of an "arbitrator" as dissension among elements on the campus has increased. The presidency, in turn, is affected by both these developments—external criticism and internal conflict—but also by increased administrative complexity and financial stringency, among other factors. Boards are more troubled. Presidents have shorter tenure—they are often the lightning rods for their campuses.

As we seek solutions, we believe that certain historical features and results of the system of governance of higher education in the United States merit preservation and enlargement, including:

- A reasonable degree of independence from state and federal control
- Institutional separation from partisan political activity
- Essential academic freedom for faculty members and students
- Essential faculty influence over academic affairs
- Availability of many options from among which students may choose in selecting their campuses, their periods of attendance, their fields of study, and their courses
- Diversity among institutions
- Adaptability to changing circumstances
- A reasonable degree of consent within the campus
- A reasonable degree of public support externally

3. General Considerations Affecting Governance

Governance of higher education is an exceedingly intricate matter. The internal practice of governance varies by type of institution—for example, faculty authority tends to be comparatively great at the leading research institutions and at the academically most prestigious liberal arts colleges. It varies by size of campus, and the small campus is more likely to constitute a face-to-face "community." It varies by control, and the private institution usually has more freedom of movement, if it wishes to exercise it, with fewer outside checks and balances. It varies by the nature of its student body, and a campus with more left-oriented students tends to be more activist in external political activity, and students tend to be more insistent internally on a participatory role. It varies by the composition of its faculty, and a "cosmopolitan" faculty tends to be more oriented both toward external political affairs and toward professional contacts across the nation. It varies by the public visibility of the campus, and the highly visible campus is a better vehicle for political activism internally and political intrusion externally since it attracts media attention. It varies by whether the campus is or is not part of a multicampus system.

Governance takes many forms and occurs in many environments. What can be said and be true about one place may not be true about another. What may be wise action in one situation may be unwise in another. The recognition of the great variety of patterns, conditions, and responses is the beginning of wisdom in approaching the problems of governance.

No clear theory about governance within institutions of higher education is generally accepted as a basis for approaching policy, and this, additionally, complicates an examination of the subject. Given both the teacher-to-student relationship

13

and the legitimate interests of many groups other than teachers and students, the campus does not lend itself to a one-man–one-vote, self-contained democracy of teachers and students. Teachers are placed in a special relationship by their more proven scholarly accomplishments. The campus is not a political democracy where all persons have identical status and rights. Nor, particularly given the professional standing of its faculty members, does the campus lend itself to a strongly corporate, hierarchical, top-down method of governance. Alternatively, the students might be viewed as sovereign consumers, but here, at least in the teacher-to-student relationship, the consumer can hardly always be considered right if standards are to be maintained —some "consumers" in such a situation will want a poorer, or at least easier to obtain, and not a better, and harder to obtain, academic product. Or, the faculty might be viewed as a fully self-governing guild, but such an approach would theoretically deny any superior public interests and any strong role for consumer influence, and could actually lead to self-serving irresponsibility unchecked by other powers. Some parts of a campus may be operated on a democratic basis, such as student government; some parts on a corporate basis, such as business affairs; some parts as a partial market, such as course offerings determined in part on the basis of student enrollments; and some parts as a guild, such as authority over course content, grades, and research projects. But not all parts can be governed in accordance with any one of these views.

Internal governance in practice has not followed a single consistent theoretical pattern; rather, it has usually related to the particular functions being performed—many diverse functions have given rise to many diverse forms of governance: the classroom is run one way, accounting another, and student extracurricular activities still another. We consider this diversity in patterns of governance both inevitable and to a degree desirable, given the many quite varied functions performed on a complex campus. We see no single clear and universal theoretical approach to governance that can or should rule unquestioned. We believe, instead, that governmental methods should be related to the specific functions being performed; should vary in total pattern as the constellations of functions vary. Central coordination of governmental methods, however, is highly necessary, and we shall suggest later that this is a basic role of the board of trustees.

With these caveats and observations in mind—the variety of situations and the absence of any single organizing principle—we call attention to the following considerations affecting governance and the suggested directions for improvement:

- Size of an institution adds to complexity and formality. We have earlier recommended "points of reassessment" in relation to size (Carnegie Commission, 1971*a*).

- Excessive aggregation of functions also adds complexity and can compound problems. First, some activities may better be eliminated altogether or turned over to semi-independent, quasi-university agencies, or to private enterprise or to cooperatives. The "company town," for example—where the same person is employer, merchant, policeman, landlord, mayor —has not worked well in industrial relations, and the "company town" approach on campus has somewhat the same effect of concentrating power and thus grievances against the wielder of that power. Second, differentiation of functions among institutions reduces the tendency toward the undue aggregation of functions in any single institution.

- Strong centralization of authority in multicampus systems or on large campuses can delay decisions and make them less responsive to specific problems. Reasonable decentralization to the campus level within multicampus systems (Lee & Bowen, 1971) and to professional schools and "cluster colleges" within large campuses can accelerate and personalize the making of many decisions.

- Where there is greater opportunity for freedom of choice or where more options are offered to individuals if complete freedom of choice is not possible (as in curricular offerings), the burden that is placed on the organized decision-making process may be reduced (Carnegie Commission, 1970*a*; 1972*a*).

- Open hearings on codes of rights and responsibilities and on other major matters of policy can give expression to diverse points of view and inform the decision-making process.

- The more attention that is given to the needs of individuals and of special minority groups (Carnegie Commission, 1970*b*), the fewer are the complaints that are likely to be directed against the processes of governance in the longer run. In the shorter run, of course, disputes over the content and control of such adjustments are likely to increase the pressures on governmental processes. Special groups that are often neglected on the campus, in addition to racial minorities and women, are the "marginals" who are not fully in one role or another —such as the teaching assistant who is both teacher and graduate student, the part-time lecturer not on the "ladder" who is a teacher but not a full faculty member, and the research person who is not a member of the faculty. They are neither fully in nor fully out.

- Some campuses have a Kafkaesque character —an uncertainty about who can make what decisions and on what grounds. Who are the judges? Where is the "Castle"? It is important to clarify who has what authority and what policies are to be followed, and to set forth for all to see where answers can be obtained. An effective administration is better than a confusing anarchy.

- Statements of rights and responsibilities, particularly in large organizations, can be helpful in clarifying relationships (Carnegie Commission, 1971*b*; 1972*a*). They are also essential to the effective conduct of formal judicial procedures. With the decline of consensus on campus and the rise of more vocal dissent toward society, such codes (regretfully) become more necessary.

- Faculty members and students should have a full measure of academic freedom, substantially as defined by the American Association of University Professors (see Appendix D).

- Faculty senates and councils should have essentially the authority recommended by the American Association of University Professors (see Appendix D).

- Staff members who are at the counters, across the desks, and on the phones, with students, faculty members, and the public are of key importance in handling problems with clarity, accuracy, and a spirit of helpfulness.

- Adequate grievance machinery, ending—for particularly difficult cases—in fully impartial tribunals not composed entirely of close colleagues and associates, is essential (Carnegie Commission, 1971*b*). The creation of the office of ombudsman has generally proven to be highly successful in the informal handling of grievances.

These several comments relate to certain of the continuing circumstances, issues, and policies that surround governance and indicate some directions for improvement in some situations.

Some major new issues, as well as many old ones, confront academic governance. We shall be concerned next with six such issues that are now a source of more lively interest than in any earlier period in the history of higher education in the United States.

4. Intellectual, Academic, and Administrative Independence

The independence of the campus from external authority has declined significantly since World War II and particularly over the past decade—more coordinating councils and superboards at the state level, more gubernatorial and legislative investigation and intrusion into once internal affairs, more federal regulations and supervision. This decline has affected both public and private institutions. A crisis of substantial importance has developed.

It is customary to speak of campus "autonomy," but there is no such thing in any full sense of the word. Full autonomy is always limited by the general law and often also by the charter of the institution. Increasingly it is also limited by state and federal influence and control. As a matter of fact, while "autonomy" is much demanded in principle, much of higher education is actually trying to escape from the remaining provinces of full financial autonomy as fast as it can. Colleges and universities avidly want more public financial support and thus must accept some dependence. Autonomy, in the sense of full self-governance, does not now exist for American higher education, nor has it existed for a very long time—if ever. Autonomy is limited by the law, by the necessary influences and controls that go along with financial support, and by public policy in areas of substantial public concern. Autonomy in these areas is neither possible nor generally desirable.

Institutional independence, however, can be and should be preserved in other areas: (1) the intellectual, through the protection of academic freedom of expression and of free choice and conduct of research projects by faculty members and students; (2) the academic, through acceptance of decision making by academic authorities in specified academic areas such as conduct

17

of courses; and (3) the administrative, through allowing substantial leeway in handling financial and personnel matters in detail.

Autonomy, in the sense of total absence of support or control, is generally neither sought by higher education nor can it be given by public authority. Higher education, however, should be substantially self-governing in its:

- Intellectual conduct
- Academic affairs
- Administrative arrangements

We should thus like to distinguish these three areas, where a substantial degree of independence is essential, from any generalized demand for total autonomy at all times and in all affairs. Selective independence—not autonomy—is the issue as we see it.

We prefer, thus, to speak of the essential independence of academic authorities within the context of public policy. We define academic authorities as being the governing agencies of the self-standing campus or of the multicampus system. We do not seek to define the relations between the component campus and the system, except to support maximum feasible decentralization.[1] We do seek, rather, to clarify the relations between the campus (or system) and external public agencies such as state coordinating councils, state legislatures, the governor's office, federal agencies, and the national Congress.

We should also like to distinguish between external influence and external control. Influence can be and has been exerted by providing special funds for special activities—and these funds can and do serve as a great magnet for campus activity—or by creating a climate of public opinion that may either encourage or discourage certain campus actions, or by direct persuasion. But influence is not control.

Control exists when an order can be given to do or not to do some certain thing with penalties attached for noncompliance. For example, the Land-Grant Act of 1862 was an example of influence—it provided an attractive idea and some resources,

---

[1] We have earlier generally favored the creation of local boards within multicampus systems (Carnegie Commission, 1971c).

but did not require any action; the action by a state legislature in specifying faculty teaching loads is control—it requires compliance.

Influence recognizes freedom of action, while control limits freedom of action. Control involves mandatory external decisions; influence permits nonmandatory internal decisions. Influence means to persuade and to reward; control means to direct and to command. Influence and control lie on a continuum—there are many borderline situations. But the essential difference is substantial, and it is important, though difficult, to distinguish where unwarranted control takes the place of permissible influence. The coercive power of the state is different in kind as well as in degree from influence, however persuasive—different both legally and psychologically.

This is not to suggest that influence has not been and cannot be of great importance. The Land-Grant Act enormously affected higher education in the United States. Federal funds in the Great Depression led to a great era of building residence halls, student unions, and other facilities. Federal funds, particularly during and after World War II, led to an enormous expansion of research activity and Ph.D. training. Federal funding incentives for offering a three-year M.D. degree are currently leading to widespread conversion to the shorter program. Influence may be effective, but it stops short of control. It is essentially positive, not negative, in its inducements. It relies upon rewards, not punishments; on persuasion, not orders.

To the extent that public authority relies upon influence and not control, institutions of higher education must rely upon their own wisdom in selecting among whatever alternatives are made available. And they must rely upon the courage of their convictions in saying "no." The restraint of public authority in not insisting must be matched by the restraint of higher education in not always seizing upon each opportunity offered even when money is attached to it. Harvard, for example, never has accepted secret research projects.

Independence from government was once an issue only for public institutions. Now that private institutions are equally subject to federal legislation and increasingly are covered by state legislation, institutional independence has become an issue for all institutions. Increasingly all institutions will have more nearly the same degree of concern.

The crisis over independence has risen quite quickly since World War II. Prior to that time, and particularly in the period after World War I, the great issue of principle had been academic freedom. The rules about academic freedom are now generally well accepted, and the mechanisms to protect it are well established, although its protection requires eternal vigilance. Institutional independence is now replacing academic freedom as a great unresolved issue of principle.

There have long been concerns about independence, particularly for state institutions—the Dartmouth College Case of 1819 established the basic independence of private institutions from public control. Issues involving independence were particularly intense for many of the new land-grant universities and colleges after the Civil War. They were torn by a struggle for independence against the populist pressures of the times for "trade" courses and "applied" research, and against political domination of the campus. Most of these battles were won by the universities and colleges over a period of decades.

The new concern over independence reflects these developments (among others):

- The rise of expenditures on higher education in one decade from 1.1 to 2.5 percent of GNP, and the prospect that they may rise to an even higher percentage

- The recent increase of dissent and disruption and the growth of new and nonconformist lifestyles on campus

- The enhanced public attention to the actual and potential contributions of higher education in solving social problems: research for better health, more wealth and welfare, more secure national defense; greater opportunities to attend and to make progress within college for members of low-income and minority racial and ethnic groups, and for women; and training facilities for urgently needed skills—recently mostly for teachers and scientists, and now mostly for health care personnel

- The transition from elite to mass to universal-access higher education, which has meant that more members of the public both care about and know about higher education

- The higher percentage of students in public as compared with private institutions

- The addition of more, and also more skilled, staff analysts—particularly in the offices of governors and state legislative instrumentalities, and in the federal government

- The centralization of data through the use of computers making possible more centralized decision making

- The creation of coordinating councils or superboards—by now in almost every state and with increasing authority

- The introduction of new federal programs on top of existing state controls

- The general ascension throughout American society, affecting corporations and trade unions and campuses, of public policy control over once, more autonomous, private interests—this is true in many other countries as well

We do not believe that the impact of this total set of forces will be much diminished in the future—more likely the opposite, although some individual forces will rise in intensity as others fall. Among those that may fall are: a lesser concern for manpower skills as deficits increasingly disappear, a lesser interest in university research if more of it is transferred to nonacademic institutions, and a lesser concern for disruption if disruption continues at a low level. Most of the other forces, however, will persist or increase in their intensity. Thus, we conclude that the problem of independence is already serious and is likely to become even more so.

Looked at very broadly, across North America and Western Europe and back to the early universities in Europe, independence of institutions of higher education has generally gained historically as against the church and as against the autocratic ruler. The church became both less powerful and more tolerant. Autocratic rulers gave way to democracies, first in the towns. Individual freedom advanced. Higher education gained in status, and institutions grew in size and complexity of functions. Other countervailing sources of support and money for higher education developed, particularly in North America— support from industry, agriculture, the professions, and the alumni. The university became a more independent unit within the increasingly more pluralistic society.

In both North America and Western Europe, however, this long historical process recently has been generally undergoing a reversal, and institutional independence is currently declining. There has been a general loss of respect and of privileged position. Higher education increasingly is taking on a public utility status subject to regulation in the name of the public interest. World War II and the subsequent period of the spread of mass higher education marked a turning point in the history of campus autonomy. The once more autonomous and more class-oriented institution is being transformed into the more publicly controlled and more mass-oriented institution.

The long-term trend of increasing institutional independence may now be giving way to a new trend of decreasing independence.

WHY INDEPENDENCE? No Holy Writ gives higher education a right to reasonable independence for institutional actions. No natural law confers upon it escape from public surveillance. The case for reasonable independence must be made with reasonable arguments.

Three common arguments are at least partially lacking in adequate merit to fully justify independence. One is that independence gives rise to diversity. It has done so in the past under conditions of considerable geographic and religious pluralism, but it may in the future almost equally give rise to the most abject imitation of others or to competitive uniformity. Differentiation of functions and specialization of subject matter among campuses, under modern circumstances, are often more likely to flow from thoughtful central planning than from independent actions, and diversity of style can, and in some cases does, result from central planning as well as from local desire. A second argument is that institutional independence leads to freedom to innovate. But the record on innovation of unfettered higher education is not outstanding—in fact, historically, many and perhaps most of the major structural innovations have been largely initiated externally, like the land-grant movement and the introduction of large-scale scientific research. A third reason often given is that the academic freedom of faculty members depends upon institutional independence. Often, it is true that the two have been associated. But academic freedom, as in Germany from Humboldt to the advent of Hitler, can be substantial although the university administratively is essentially an arm of the state. Nor has academic freedom in the United States suffered because of the recent decline in campus independence. Institutional independence often may be helpful to a spirit of academic freedom and to the protection of that freedom against external attack, but it does not guarantee such freedom, and academic freedom may exist in the absence of substantial campus independence if supported by the law and by public opinion.

These three standard arguments, on examination, do not, by themselves, make a sufficiently clear case for independence. Other reasons for independence are:

- Professional matters are best left to members of the profession. This is basic. Thus the professional faculty and the professional administrators, under the aegis of informed trustees, are best qualified to define merit in the selection of individual students to be admitted to a campus, to select and promote faculty members on the basis of their academic ability, to approve courses and determine content, to undertake and approve research projects, to approve the awarding of individual degrees, to distribute money for these purposes in detail, and to select departmental leadership.

- Reasonable independence improves the spirit of the campus, the sense of responsibility of faculty members, students, administrators, and trustees, and the devotion of members of these key groups to its welfare. Only with a sense of local responsibility and of devotion among these central groups to their own institution can a campus be fully effective. The spirit of academic free enterprise has parallels with the spirit of economic free enterprise in eliciting effort and accountability.

- Reasonable independence draws forth more advice and more funds from alumni and friends than does excessive control by the state. As Tocqueville so well described, part of the genius of American society is found in its ability to draw on the interest and goodwill of individual citizens through voluntary effort.

- Reasonable independence reduces the likelihood of the intrusion of partisan politics and of a "spoils" system into the administration of higher education, reduces the weight of bureaucracy and the number of layers of administration with the extra delays and costs that such additional layers involve and the sense of irresponsibility at lower levels that they encourage, and reduces the uncertainty that goes along with changing political leadership. Higher education is more likely to be effective if it stands largely outside changing and partisan politics, and remains largely unburdened by governmental bureaucracy.

- Higher education provides, through its faculty members and students, one of the checks and balances in a democratic society, along with a free press, a free church, and the three-fold split into executive, legislative, and judicial authority. Individual members of campus communities should be fully free to study, to evaluate, to advise on the conduct of other institutions in society. This "checks-and-balances" or "critical" function is more likely to be performed adequately if there is a reasonable degree of independence than if there is not—witness the Soviet Union. Academic freedom will protect the individual dissenter, but beyond such individual dissent there needs to be affirmative institutional support for constructive evaluation and advice. The institution-as-such should not take political positions about external affairs, but it should be committed to a checks-and-balances function for its individual faculty members and students. This function requires reasonable independence for the institution as well as essential freedoms for its members.

- Historical experience shows that the best of the colleges and universities, in academic terms, have generally been among those with the greater institutional independence—the private institutions and the freer of the state institutions. Independence does not assure quality, but academic quality is less likely without independence.

- Control by the state means responsibility by the state. Campus crises then can become governmental crises. In France, a nationalized system of higher education has led to great political crises that could have been reduced in their intensity if the universities had been more independent. The national government there had responsibility for the total conduct of higher education and not just for the maintenance of law and order.

Thus the case for independence largely rests on the professional nature of many of the decisions that must be made, on the need to elicit the devotion and sense of responsibility of the major groups internally involved, on the wisdom of drawing advice and support from interested private citizens, on the costs of partisan political and bureaucratic intrusions, on the desirability of having the campus community as one of the checks-and-balances in our pluralistic society, and on the experience of history on what works best both academically and politically.

Independence may be warranted, but its preservation is not easy. The churches gained their independence by forgoing state financial support. The campuses want to keep their independence while retaining and even increasing their state financial support. This is more difficult.

EARNING INDEPENDENCE Control usually follows money, and more money is now coming from public sources. How then may independence be earned? We suggest that it may be earned by:

- Performing, at a high level of quality, functions that are important to the people in the larger society

- Demonstrating capacity for effective self-governance
- Making effective use of the resources provided by society
- Abiding by the law on campus
- Assuring *institutional* neutrality in partisan politics and in public controversies external to the institution
- Preserving its own intellectual integrity from attacks from within as well as from without
- Giving full and honest explanations, to the public in general, and to legislators and elected administrators in particular, about all matters of broad public concern

The public interest, in turn, is largely served by these same means. The public has an interest in the rule of law, in useful functions well-performed, in effective use of resources, in responsible self-governance, in institutional neutrality, in intellectual integrity, and in adequate information. The better these interests are served, the more willingness there will be to confer independence.

A long-run purpose of higher education is to aid the people in the wider society. The purpose of public support for higher education, on the other hand, is not to aid faculty members or administrators to serve their own self-interests when these depart from socially useful functions. The higher education community earns independence by what it does in the public interest, not by what it does for itself alone or by what it demands for itself alone. It has no inherent right, regardless of its conduct, to support and independence.

DISTRIBUTION OF AUTHORITY To achieve balance between public control and influence versus institutional independence, the Commission favors the following patterns for the distribution of authority between public agencies (including coordinating councils) and academic institutions (including multicampus systems):

PUBLIC CONTROL	INSTITUTIONAL INDEPENDENCE
Governance	
Basic responsibility for law enforcement	
Right to insist on political neutrality of *institutions* of higher education	Right to refuse oaths not required of all citizens in similar circumstances

PUBLIC CONTROL	INSTITUTIONAL INDEPENDENCE

Governance

Duty to appoint trustees of public institutions of higher education (or to select them through popular election)	Right to independent trustees: No ex officio regents with subsequent budgetary authority
	Right to nonpartisan trustees as recommended by some impartial screening agency, or as confirmed by some branch of the state legislature, or both; or as elected by the public
Right to reports and accountability on matters of public interest	
Duty of courts to hear cases alleging denial of general rights of a citizen and of unfair procedures	

Financial and Business Affairs

Appropriation of public funds on basis of general formulas that reflect quantity and quality of output	Assignment of all funds to specific purposes
Postaudit, rather than preaudit, of expenditures, of purchases, of personnel actions	Freedom to make expenditures within budget, to make purchases, and to take personnel actions subject only to postaudit
Examination of effective use of resources on a postaudit basis	Determination of individual work loads and of specific assignments to faculty and staff members
Standards for accounting practices and postaudit of them	
General level of salaries	Determination of specific salaries
Appropriation of public funds for buildings on basis of general formulas for building requirements	Design of buildings and assignment of space

Academic and Intellectual Affairs

General policies on student admissions:	Selection of individual students
Number of places	
Equality of access	
Academic level of general eligibility among types of institutions	

PUBLIC CONTROL	INSTITUTIONAL INDEPENDENCE
Academic and Intellectual Affairs	

PUBLIC CONTROL	INSTITUTIONAL INDEPENDENCE
General distribution of students by level of division	
Policies for equal access to employment for women and for members of minority groups	Academic policies for, and actual selection and promotion of, faculty members
Policies on differentiation of functions among systems of higher education and on specialization by major fields of endeavor among institutions	Approval of individual courses and course content
No right to expect secret research or service from members of institutions of higher education; and no right to prior review before publication of research results; but right to patents where appropriate	Policies on and administration of research and service activities
	Determination of grades and issuance of individual degrees
	Selection of academic and administrative leadership
Enforcement of the national Bill of Rights	Policies on academic freedom
Policies on size and rate of growth of campuses	Policies on size and rate of growth of departments and schools and colleges within budgetary limitations
Establishment of new campuses and other major new endeavors, such as a medical school, and definition of scope	Academic programs for new campuses and other major new endeavors within general authorization

INFLUENCE BUT NOT PUBLIC CONTROL	INSTITUTIONAL INDEPENDENCE
Academic Affairs—Innovation	
Encouragement of innovation through inquiry, recommendation, allocation of special funds, application of general budgetary formulas, starting new institutions	Development of and detailed planning for innovation

The problem of innovation is a particularly difficult one. A public interest does exist in the adaptation of higher education to social needs, as in the case of the land-grant movement. But innovations will not work well unless there is acceptance of them by those who will be responsible for their actual introduction and operation. Thus cooperative effort is a better mechanism than executive or legislative order, although these may occasionally be required. Taking as an illustration the interest of several states in the possibility of a three-year option for students seeking the B.A. degree, we suggest that the interest of the appropriate officials be pursued by first requesting a study by institutions of higher education and later, if necessary, by making a recommendation to them. Or they may provide a special bonus for three-year degrees as the federal government has done for the three-year medical degree, or assume in budgetary allocations that a certain percentage of degrees will be on a three-year basis (or, at the Ph.D. level, by subsidizing education only for a four- or five-year period for each student, after which no allowance is made for the student in the allocation of public funds for operating costs or space utilization), or they may create new institutions on this basis. Generally, the less the control the better. Persuasiveness and ingenuity in exerting influence are better than direct orders. Thus we list academic innovation under influence but not control.

The method of funding affects independence. We have favored and continue to favor providing federal funds in the form of grants or loans to students rather than as bloc grants to institutions, thus making the students into more of a market force and reducing the likelihood of direct governmental control; research funds given on the merit of specific applications rather than as bloc grants to institutions; and reliance of institutions on several federal agencies rather than on one alone.

To preserve independence requires not only appropriate policies but also some agency to review the application of these policies, as has the American Association of University Professors in the area of academic freedom. We repeat our suggestion that the American Council on Education establish a Commission on Institutional Independence to be concerned with policies affecting independence and with the degree of adherence to them (Carnegie Commission, 1971c). We make this suggestion, in part, because there has been a substantial sphere of ambiguity in the past. The campus largely occupied this sphere by default. As governmental authority has expanded, however, it has moved increasingly into these areas and occupied them. The ambiguities that were once an asset are now a liability. Greater precision of understanding is now highly desirable.

Recommendation 1: State grants to institutions for general support should be based on broad formulas and not line-item control.

Recommendation 2: Academic policies set by state agencies should be of a broad nature and should not interfere with the more specific professional academic judgments about faculty appointments, courses of study, admission of individual students, grades and degrees for individual students, specific research projects, appointment of academic and administrative staff and leadership, and protection of academic freedom.

Recommendation 3: Innovations in programs and in policies should be encouraged by public authorities by influence and not by control.

Recommendation 4: Coordinating agencies at the state level should seek to establish, in cooperation with public and private institutions of higher education, guidelines defining areas of state concern and areas of institutional independence that avoid detailed control.

Recommendation 5: The American Council on Education may wish to consider establishing a Commission on Institutional Independence to be concerned with policies affecting independence and the review of cases of alleged undue external influence. Such a Commission should include members drawn from the public at large.

An effort to assure essential institutional independence— such as the one waged for essential academic freedoms, beginning half a century ago, by the American Association of University Professors —is now necessary. But in this effort, the academic community should realize that public initiative has had, and can have, good as well as bad results, and that it may be needed in the future to protect the campus from internal attacks on academic freedom even though public interference once was and may again be a major source of threat to academic freedom.

The discussion above has related mostly to public institutions, but to the extent that private institutions become more subject to public policy, we believe that the same general principles should apply.

5. Providing for Governance— The Role of the Board and of the President

The board of trustees once governed the institution in detail. It represented the denominational church that originated the campus, or a well-defined cultural model of "Western civilization," or both. It knew what it wanted in the socialization of students to moral beliefs and/or cultural behavior. But the role of the church has declined; acculturation is now carried on by many agencies and groups—including the student peer group itself—and is directed toward no single model of man; the campus has generally become larger and, almost always, more complex; the faculty has become much more professional and much more specialized; the state has become much more involved in the fiscal operations of more institutions; and the board, as a consequence, has gradually had its control reduced. The first delegation of authority by the board to the president in the history of the University of California came in 1891 when the president was permitted to hire a janitor, provided he reported his action promptly to the board. Much has happened to board control since that day.

The board was dominant until the period of the Civil War. Its controlling influence then increasingly gave way to that of the president, particularly to the powerful presidents who modernized American higher education at Harvard, Cornell, Johns Hopkins, Michigan, Wisconsin, Stanford, California, and elsewhere, and who, in turn, became the models for presidents everywhere. The era of presidential dominance continued until about the time of World War I. Then faculties began to assert their influence more and more until about 1960, when the students became more active and, particularly, when the states began to assert their authority more strongly. Where once stood the authority of the board alone, now stood the president, the faculty, the students, and the state, plus a board now often greatly diminished in its operational authority—with the major exception of many of the community colleges. Some observers, viewing these historical trends, have predicted the demise of the board altogether; some have even recommended its rapid disappearance as an unnecessary artifact of an earlier age.

But the board, in our judgment, continues to be an essential institution in higher education. It is not just the best of several unsatisfactory alternatives. It has, in the United States, provided generally good governance for higher education, as witnessed by the growth in the quantity and quality of endeavors, by the diversity among campuses, by the adaptability of the system to new circumstances, and by its comparative independence from governmental domination. The board is essential, in part, also by default—no other mechanism can provide for governance so well, not the state, not the faculty, not the students, and not the faculty and the students together. State control, as seen in many nations, tends to become both too bureaucratic and too representative of what society wants; the faculty is not generally chosen for its administrative talents and is divided administratively by its own special interests; the students are inexperienced and transient; and the students and the faculty are in certain significant disagreements about influence over academic matters, as we shall discuss subsequently.

The board, at its best, serves these functions:

- It holds and interprets the "trust"—the responsibility for the long-run welfare of the total institution; it defines the purposes to be followed and the standards to be met; it is the guardian of the mission of the campus; it evaluates overall performance.

- It acts as a "buffer" between society and the campus, resisting improper external interference and introducing a necessary contact with the changing realities of the surrounding society; it is the principal gatekeeper for the campus, and its judgment about what is improper interference on the one hand, and what is constructive adjustment on the other, is of the utmost importance to the conduct of the institution.

- It is the final arbiter of internal disputes involving the administration, the faculty, and the students—the court of last resort for most disagreements.

- It is an "agent of change," in what is historically a conservative institution, deciding what changes should be permitted and what changes should be encouraged and when. The great period of modernization a century ago took place under the supervision and with the concurrence of the then existing boards; so have other major changes since that time.

- It has the basic responsibility for the financial welfare of the campus.

- Above all, it provides for the governance of the institution—even if it no longer actively governs in detail; it appoints and removes the president and other chief officers, and arranges for the administrative structure.

These roles are important at any time; they are more than usually important under current circumstances, when purposes are being reexamined, when the essential independence of the campus is being eroded, when conflict on campus has intensified, when change is more than normally necessary, and when governance has become so much more difficult. The role of the board of trustees is due for a renaissance.[1]

To perform its functions well, the board needs to be independent, free of conflict of interest, competent, devoted, and sensitive to the interests of the several groups involved in the life of the campus. Thus we oppose politically elected officials serving ex officio on boards of public institutions because they both reduce the independence of the campus from state control and introduce a conflict of interest due to their necessary political partisanship; and, since they later act on budgets and other major policies, they have a major opportunity for influence and a major measure of control in any event (Carnegie Commission, 1971c).

We also oppose faculty members and students of an institution serving on the board of *the same institution* because of potential conflicts of interest, and also because it is difficult to assure that they really are "representative" of the faculty or the student body—if "representatives" are what is wanted (which we greatly doubt). Additionally, such membership would more likely draw board attention to day-to-day specific actions. Also, as we shall note later, the trend toward unionization of faculty members raises additional questions about their service on boards. And the trend for students to establish their own lob-

---

[1] This view, we realize, runs counter to much of faculty opinion. Nearly one-half of faculty members recently surveyed agreed strongly or with reservations that the "Trustees' only responsibility should be to raise money and gain community support" (see Appendix A, Table A-6). We consider this an unwisely narrow view of the role of the board.

bies at state legislatures raises questions about their service on boards. We do favor having faculty members and students serve either on appropriate committees of the board or on parallel committees that meet with board committees—the choice between these two approaches will depend greatly on the history and the nature of the individual institution. Such consultation through the committee work of the board can add both to the wisdom of decisions and to the sense of legitimacy of the decision-making process.

We favor some impartial screening device for nomination of members of public boards, or legislative confirmation of appointments, or some combination of both. We also favor providing an opportunity for faculty members, students, and alumni to assist in the nomination of at least some board members in both private and public institutions—all for the sake of securing devoted and competent members. We also favor broad inclusion of persons interested in the welfare of the institution drawn from different age, sex, and racial groups in order to represent concerns of the different groups that hold an attachment to the campus, so that a greater variety of perspectives is brought to board deliberations. And we specifically favor the consideration of faculty members from other institutions and of young alumni as board members.

Thus we support the concept of an impartial board as against one that represents special external or internal interests. There should be no "delegates" with special mandates. The board is the ultimate protector of the long-run welfare of the total institution. To serve effectively as a buffer externally and as an arbitrator internally, the board can neither reflect external partisanship nor internal interests. To handle conflict well, it must itself be neutral; it must be "above the battle," not partisan within it. It must be as impartial as possible about everything except its trust. Also, as an agent of change, it should not be committed to the internal status quo.

Since many boards do not meet the principles we recommend, they are due for a reformation in their composition as well as for a renaissance of their influence.

Recommendation 6: Elected officials with the power of budgetary review should not serve as members of governing boards of public institutions over which they exercise such review because of the conflict of interest and the resulting double access to control, and because of the partisan nature of their positions.

Recommendation 7: Members of governing boards of public institutions (where the governor makes the appointments) should be subject to appropriate mechanisms for nominating and screening individuals before appointment by the governor to assure consideration of properly qualified individuals, or to subsequent legislative confirmation to reduce the likelihood of purely politically partisan appointments, or to both.

Recommendation 8: Faculty members, students, and alumni should be associated with the process of nominating at least some board members in private and public institutions, but faculty members and students should not serve on the boards of institutions where they are enrolled or employed.

Recommendation 9: Board membership should reflect the different age, sex, and racial groups that are involved in the concerns of the institution. Faculty members from other institutions and young alumni should be considered for board memberships.

Recommendation 10: Boards should consider faculty and student membership on appropriate board committees, or the establishment of parallel committees with arrangements for joint consultation.

Recommendation 11: Boards periodically should review the arrangements for governance—perhaps every four or five years—to be certain that they fit the current needs of the institution and are appropriate to the various functions being performed.

Boards of trustees are particularly responsible for the areas reviewed in this report:

- To assure their own integrity and competence
- To provide for effective administrative leadership
- To define institutional goals and to assess performance

- To allocate decision-making authority in accordance with competence and responsibility

- To be certain that there are effective processes of decision making, that the arrangements for governance are sufficient but not excessive — since governance is a necessary means but not the end purpose of an academic institution

- To survey the context of governance —size of campus, combination of functions performed, centralization and decentralization of authority, definitions of rules and responsibilities, and provision of fair methods and procedures for judicial review

- To assure the long-term financial solvency of the institution

- To define and protect the essential independence of the campus, and to advocate support of its welfare

- To settle internal disputes judiciously

- To act as an agent of constructive change

- To develop an approach to faculty authority and to collective bargaining

- To provide reasonable rules governing tenure and to supervise their administration

- To incorporate students sensibly into the governance process

- To assure that emergencies can be effectively handled

It is more important for the board to provide for effective governance than, as it once did, for it to govern; it should spend more time on governance and less time on governing than it has historically. The board should neither abdicate its responsibilities to external or internal forces, nor bog itself down in the details of administration. It should not run the college, but it should assure that it is well run.

THE PRESIDENCY Under the general direction of the board, the president holds the key administrative position. He must extend leadership in relation to faculty members and other staff, students, alumni, government agencies, and the public more generally.

The position of the president has fluctuated substantially in its general degree of influence. Once largely an agent of the board, the president, particularly after the Civil War, assumed the role of dominant leader. This was a period of great change that required strong administrative direction. Then, particularly after World War I, faculty organizations began assuming more control, and it was a period, in any event, of less dramatic change. The period of great growth after World War II once again lent itself to forceful administrative leadership; but the period of the second half of the 1960s saw an erosion of presidential influence with the rise of student unrest, the expansion of the authority of state agencies, and the more rapid replacement of presidents. Now, this trend may again be undergoing a reversal. Students are more quiet. Faculty members are more tired of campus controversy and of participating in governing activities. Members of both groups seem to be more willing to let the president handle problems and make decisions. And financial stringencies almost force a president to play a more central role—as do the more clearly perceived conflicts between the "insiders"—whom he represents —versus the "outsiders" (Gross & Grambsch, forthcoming).

We believe that the present period calls for substantial changes on campus and in the relationships of the campus to society. This, in turn, will require greater presidential influence to initiate and to guide the changes. It is also a period of more than usual conflict on campus that requires understanding and action. Additionally, fiscal stringency requires more administrative authority. We believe consequently, that boards should seek to appoint active rather than passive presidents, presidents who will lead rather than just survive. They should also give presidents adequate authority and staff, and their own support in the difficult task of encouraging constructive change—realizing that periods of change are also periods of unusual tension—and of effectively resolving conflict.

The president has usually been appointed on a no-term basis—with the major exception of many community colleges where term appointments are made. He has served at the will of the board. The actual tenure of presidents is now about 6 years—half of what it once was. We believe that some presidents would be aided if a review period were agreed upon in advance so that a more normal opportunity than now exists would be created for mutual reassessment of the situation and of the president's performance. Many deans and department chairmen now serve on just this basis. This should in no way, however, interfere with necessary emergency actions by the board or by the president.

Recommendation 12: Boards should seek active presidents and give them the authority and the staff they need to provide leadership in a period of change and conflict.

Recommendation 13: Boards may wish to consider the establishment of stated review periods for presidents so that withdrawal by the president or reaffirmation of the president may be managed in a more effective manner than is often now the actual situation. Faculty members and students should be associated in an advisory capacity with the process of review as they are in the initial appointment.[2]

Overall, we support, particularly under current circumstances, the concepts of an effective board and an active president.

[2] American Association of University Professors, March 4, 1972 (Appendix D).

6. Collective Bargaining and Faculty Power

The 1960s were marked by student dissent and student organization. The 1970s may equally be marked by faculty dissent and faculty organization. The decade of the student may be followed by the decade of the faculty. The locus of activism is shifting. Faculties have much to be concerned about:

- Salaries are rising more slowly; real income, in some instances, has actually been reduced.

- Budgetary support for faculty interests is much harder to obtain.

- More efforts are being made to control conditions of employment, such as workload.

- Students have intruded into what were once faculty preserves for decision making, and these intrusions and their possible extension are a source of worry for many faculty members.

- External authorities, outside the reach of faculty influence, are making more of the decisions that affect the campus and the faculty.

- Policies on promotion and tenure are more of an issue both as the rate of growth of higher education slows down, thus making fewer opportunities available, and as women and members of minority groups compete more actively for such opportunities as exist.

These concerns intensify the attention now being given to the possibilities of widespread extension of collective bargaining. Some state laws and the policies of the National Labor Relations Board are now more favorable to collective organization by faculty members; the doubling of the number of faculty members in the 1960s brought in many more young faculty members, who are more predisposed toward collective bargaining than their older colleagues; more nonfaculty employees are becoming organized on campus. The most rapidly growing segment of higher education—the community colleges—is the segment most closely tied to secondary education where collective bargaining is already quite extensive. Some early faculty contracts (as in the City University of New York) have included very high salary rates on a comparative basis. The situation is a volatile one.

Faculty members, at least in the more prestigious academic institutions, have long engaged in informal and discrete bargaining with administrators, individually or through their faculty committees. But faculty members, even in these institutions, are now under greater pressures than before—from students who want more power, from legislatures that have potential power and want more control, from a labor market that was most favorable but has now become relatively unfavorable. They are on the defensive. And some of them are organizing or considering organizing to defend themselves in a suddenly more hostile world and in a society where organized groups surround them. Unionization for them is more a protective than an aggressive act, more an effort to preserve the status quo than to achieve a new position of influence and affluence as has so often been the goal of unionization for other groups in earlier times.

But in many colleges, particularly in community colleges and some former teachers colleges, faculty members never have had much influence through committees and senates. For them, power is not something to be preserved but something yet to be obtained. Collective bargaining may provide them, for the first time, with an opportunity to obtain power from administrators and trustees, to equalize their authority with that of faculties in other types of institutions. And collective bargaining, with its tendency toward standardized rules, is also less of a change—or no change at all—when compared with the more varied and informal arrangements in other institutions.

Preservation of authority is a main motive in the first group of institutions; and redistribution of authority, in the second. Thus two types of situations should be distinguished: (1) where faculty members already have substantial influence and (2) where they have little or none. We place in the former group institutions where faculties have substantially the authority recommended by the American Association of University Professors (see Appendix D); and in the latter, those which do not meet these recommended standards. It is our view that faculties in most, if not all, institutions should have approximately the level of authority recommended by the American Association of University Professors. We give this a high level of priority.

Recommendation 14: Faculties should be granted, where they do not already have it, the general level of authority as recommended by the American Association of University Professors.

Unionization of faculty members is now proceeding rapidly. About 170 bargaining units including faculty members now exist (as of January 1973), involving about 250 individual institutions among the 2,800 institutions in the United States; and about three-fourths of these units are on community college campuses. Approximately 75,000 faculty members are covered by these units, as compared with 10,000 by a smaller number of units five years ago.[1] Unionization has proceeded fastest in states which permit collective bargaining for public employees, like New York, Michigan, and Hawaii; and in situations that are closest to the unions of teachers in the primary and secondary schools, as in the community colleges. Bargaining units including faculty members now cover about 15 percent of the half-million full-time-equivalent faculty positions.

But collective bargaining sentiment goes far beyond the organized units of the present time. In 1969—and pro-collective bargaining sentiment may have increased since then—the Carnegie Commission survey (see Table 1) found a little more than half of faculty members generally favoring collective bargaining in higher education and a little less than half generally accepting the idea of faculty strikes. The data (Appendix A, Tables A-7 through A-14) may be summarized as follows:

- Sentiment for unionization is strongest in community colleges and in the more specialized comprehensive colleges (usually, predominantly teachers colleges) that are closest to teachers at the secondary and primary levels, and weakest in the research universities where faculty members usually have substantial independence and authority.

- Sentiment is strongest among faculty members under 30, among non-tenured faculty members, and among those who are "left" regardless of age. The relationship to political leaning is particularly strong.

[1] Garbarino (forthcoming), updated as of January 1973.

TABLE 1 *Faculty opinions about collective bargaining and faculty strikes*

	Collective bargaining has a place in higher education (percentage agree)*	There are circumstances in which a faculty strike would be legitimate (percentage yes)†	Faculty should be more militant in defending their interests (percentage agree)‡
All faculty	59	46	55
Type of institution			
Doctoral-granting institutions			
Research and doctoral I	53	46	56
Other doctoral	55	44	55
Comprehensive colleges and universities	64	48	57
Liberal arts colleges	60	45	53
Two-year colleges	68	47	53
Age of faculty members			
Older than 50	51	32	52
41 to 50	57	44	54
31 to 40	62	52	57
30 or younger	68	59	58
Tenure status			
Tenured	55	40	53
Nontenured	64	52	57
Self-described political leaning			
Left	88	93	90
Liberal	68	61	68
Middle-of-the-road	55	37	47
Strongly or moderately conservative	45	26	37
Evaluation of institution's faculty salary levels			
Excellent or good	53	40	49
Fair or poor	64	52	60
Evaluation of effectiveness of faculty senate			
Excellent or good	54	38	46
Fair or poor	63	52	61
Evaluation of administration			
Excellent or good	53	37	45
Fair or poor	66	57	66

* Percentage responding "disagree strongly" or "disagree with reservations" that "collective bargaining by faculty members has no place in a college or university."

† Percentage responding "definitely yes" or "probably yes" that "there are circumstances in which a strike would be a legitimate means of collective action for faculty members."

‡ Percentage responding "agree strongly" or "agree with reservations" that "faculty members should be more militant in defending their interests."

SOURCE: Carnegie Commission survey, 1969.

- Sentiment for unionization is stronger among faculty members who consider their salaries low, the effectiveness of their academic senate "fair" or "poor," and the administration "fair" or "poor."

We believe that faculty members should have the right to organize and to bargain collectively, if they so desire, in both public and private institutions.

Recommendation 15: State laws, where they do not now permit it, should provide faculty members in public institutions the opportunity of obtaining collective bargaining rights. One alternative under such laws should be choice of no bargaining unit.

The Commission, as such, however, does not take a position on whether faculty members should unionize and engage in collective bargaining. We believe that this is a matter for faculty decision—"unions of their own choosing." But we also believe that faculty members should analyze very carefully whether or not they want to bargain collectively. Substantial impacts on many aspects of academic life are potentially involved. Realizing that situations vary enormously from one institution to another, we suggest that faculty members consider such matters as the following, in addition to the more immediate concerns listed earlier:

- Faculty members now often have what amounts to de facto comanagement rights in most areas of direct academic concern: courses of instruction, research projects, selection and promotion of colleagues, determination of grades and degrees, admissions, academic freedom, and selection of academic administrators. In fact, on some campuses it may be said that they have management rights in these areas subject only to occasional veto. What impact will collective bargaining have on the strength of these rights where they now exist and on the environment within which they are exercised?

- Unionization by faculty members may give rise on some campuses to unionization by students. What consequences may this have for faculty authority? It is interesting that while faculty unionization carries the connotation of a progressive alliance with the workers, it has the conservative reality of excluding students. Students may come to find that the participation they achieve in faculty-student committees is partly nullified by their exclusion from faculty bargaining units. They may seek to organize in response. This organization may be of a political rather than of a union nature, and faculty unions on campus may face student political associations at the state capitol.

- Unionization may strengthen managerial authority. Matters now actually in the hands of individual faculty members and their departments, such as determination of teaching loads, are likely to become subject to the terms of the contract; management may bargain for productivity rather than leave it, as it so often is, in the hands of the individual faculty members and departments; grievances may be placed before outside arbitrators rather than before faculty committees seeking to protect their colleagues. The attitude may come to be that managers should manage and that teachers should teach. Faculty members now have a certain amount of influence because of the ignorance, or the lack of interest, or the inadvertence of boards—all of which may erode with more formal and explicit arrangements. Collective bargaining could come to look like a management plot. "The legal and economic significance of the contract, as well as the practices of collective bargaining, requires a more activist role on the part of the board. Moreover, administrators become board agents more clearly than in the pre-union past, when a benign ambiguity prevailed" (Boyd, 1972).

- Campus autonomy will be reduced. It is a basic law of collective bargaining to settle disputes with the people who have the money. For state institutions, these people are the governors and the legislators. Thus bargaining for large systems will almost inevitably be with the governor and with legislative committees. The National Labor Relations Board, and similar state boards, will determine basic issues like the composition of the bargaining unit and the topics subject to bargaining. Arbitrators will rule on contract disputes and grievances. Also, greater line-item budgeting may be used as a defense against bargaining demands for redistribution of funds at the campus level.

- What will be the impacts on interdepartmental and intercampus uniformity, on flexibility of treatment of individual cases, on innovation, on seniority versus merit, on the tone of the relationships with administrators and trustees?

- What may be the impact of collective bargaining on the position of senior as against junior faculty members, and on faculty members generally as against nonfaculty personnel if they are combined in the same bargaining unit?

- What are prospects for use of the strike weapon? No product for, or immediate service to, society at large will be stopped by a strike. Children are less likely to be sent home to their parents, as happens when strikes occur at the elementary and secondary school level. Without great affirmative leverage through the strike, what may be the negative consequences of resort to the strike on sources of support?

These are some of the issues for consideration. Many different evaluations of them will be made.

Faculty members will need to decide more clearly what they really want by way of governing structures. Some conflicts of opinion and some ambiguities now exist (see Table 2 and Appendix A, Tables A-7, A-8, A-15, A-16, and A-17):

- Do they want to be their own trustees (as at Oxford and Cambridge) or at least share membership in the board of trustees, as 89 percent say they do (see Table 2)?

- Do they want codetermination with administrators and trustees in areas of academic concerns, as they now often have? Only 54 percent of faculty members, however, rate their administration as "good" or "excellent," and a clear majority (60 percent) rate their senate or faculty council as "fair" or "poor" (see Table 2). Thus these two major elements of codetermination—administration and senate—do not register generally strong approval. Most faculty members, however, rate their participation in and influence on departmental matters at a comparatively high level (see Table 2), and this is where most of the comanagement actually takes place. They also generally feel they have an opportunity to influence institutional policy, but to a much lesser degree.

TABLE 2 *Faculty attitudes about forms of participation in governance (in percentages)*

	*Agree**	*Disagree†*
Should be faculty representation on governing board	89	11
Collective bargaining has a place on campus	59	41
Governance should be completely by faculty and students for improvement of undergraduate education	40	60
Institution would be better off with fewer administrators	45	55

	Fair or poor	*Excellent or good*
Rate administration	46	54
Rate faculty senate or council	60	40

	None	*Some*	*Great deal or quite a bit*
Opportunity to influence departmental policy	8	32	60
Opportunity to influence institutional policy	34	48	18

*Agree "strongly" or "with reservations"

†Disagree "strongly" or "with reservations"

SOURCE: Carnegie Commission survey, 1969.

- Do they support the idea of collective bargaining with administrators and trustees? Somewhat more than half reply in the affirmative (see Table 2).

- Do they want to share power jointly with the students—40 percent say they do—at least as a method of improving undergraduate education (see Table 2)?

- Do they want to leave it all to the administration? The substantial number of "fair" and "poor" ratings for administrators would imply a negative response. And 45 percent say their institution would be better off with fewer administrators (see Table 2).

- Do they want a situation of "totalism"—where everybody gets in on everything? Faculty caution—to be noted later—about student influence over basic academic issues, like appointments and promotions, would indicate not.

- Or what combination of these possibilities do they want?

These possibilities are not all consistent with each other (see Chart 1), and their simultaneous advancement by some of the

CHART 1   *Attitudes of faculty members about collective bargaining and alternative forms of governance*

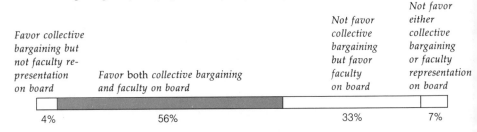

Collective bargaining and faculty representation on governing board:

Favor collective bargaining but not faculty representation on board	*Favor both collective bargaining and faculty on board*	*Not favor collective bargaining but favor faculty on board*	*Not favor either collective bargaining or faculty representation on board*
4%	56%	33%	7%

Collective bargaining and governance completely by faculty and students in order to improve undergraduate education:

Favor collective bargaining but not governance by faculty and students	*Favor both collective bargaining and governance by faculty and students*	*Not favor collective bargaining but favor faculty and student governance*	*Not favor either collective bargaining or governance by faculty and students*
32%	28%	12%	28%

SOURCE: Carnegie Commission survey, 1969.

same individuals indicates a substantial degree of confusion. Collective bargaining is not fully consistent with holding membership on the board of trustees—sitting on both sides of the bargaining table—yet 93 percent of those who favor collective bargaining also favor faculty representation on the board of trustees (see Appendix A, Table A-18). Codetermination and trustee membership are more compatible with each other than are collective bargaining and trustee membership. Also, faculty members are more likely to participate in the choice of administrators, such as deans and presidents, under codetermination than under collective bargaining. Faculty-student syndicalism is incompatible with the existence of trustees at all, and thus with collective bargaining with the trustees—yet 47 percent of faculty members who favor collective bargaining also support complete governance by the faculty and students together, at least for the sake of its impact on the improvement of undergraduate education (see Appendix A, Table A-18). And the problems of such joint governance will be intense if faculty members continue their sense of caution about sharing voting rights with students on important academic matters.

There are several routes to power, but they cannot all be followed simultaneously. Faculty members are now quite ambivalent about administrators, about their own senates, about collective bargaining, about student power; and generally uncertain about how they may best exert their own power. It is easier to support a generally "militant" approach (see Table 1) than to select the specific means of expression for this militancy. At some point, rhetoric and sentiment will need to give way to reality, and hard decisions will need to be made. Greater clarification is clearly in order.

The basic choice at the present time, we believe, is among (1) codetermination and (2) collective bargaining, or (3) some combination between the two where codetermination is effective in some subject-matter areas (such as the curriculum) and collective bargaining in others (such as salaries). This latter alternative may not turn out to be a possible combination in the longer run, however, because collective bargaining may tend to supplant codetermination in an irreversible process. And it should be clearly understood that faculty members cannot have it both ways—they cannot engage in codetermination and in collective bargaining on the same issues at the same time.

Recommendation 16: Faculties in each institution should undertake the most careful analysis of the implications of collective bargaining and, more broadly, of which of the alternative forms of governance they prefer.

This Commission believes that, at least in some situations, current arrangements will be deemed preferable to major changes.

Some faculties have chosen collective bargaining. Many others, attracted by the prospects of higher salaries, better and more certain conditions, more control over the institution, and other prospective gains, will make this same choice. Two particularly difficult questions then arise: First, should they favor a narrow or a broad unit of representation—faculty members only or also other or even all employees? And, second, should they favor narrow or broad contracts in terms of coverage—salaries and other economic benefits only, or also academic and financial and governance policies?

The unit issue is a difficult one, particularly on large campuses and in research universities. The broader the unit is, the more power it is likely to have; but the narrower it is, the more it will respond to faculty interests. We favor the narrow unit. Faculty members constitute a separate professional craft that differentiates them clearly from other employees. They usually also have managerial responsibilities over hiring and firing, over courses, grades and degrees, over teaching assistants and other staff members, and over many other matters. Additionally, faculty members have special conditions, like sabbatical leaves, that do not apply to other employees. Moreover, faculty interests can be overwhelmed in comprehensive units, and they are too central to the welfare of the institution to be overwhelmed.

It is of the utmost importance to realize that the bargaining unit, whatever it may be—whether faculty only or an entire campus or an entire system—will tend to become coterminus with the authority unit. Whichever unit (the bargaining unit or the authority unit) is at the broader and higher level of centralization, the other unit tends to match it. Especially difficult problems may develop where different types of institutions (such as a community college and a research university) are included in the same system.

Other groups of employees should, of course, have the right to bargain collectively through their own units if they so choose.

Recommendation 17: Representation and bargaining units should be composed of faculty members, including department chairmen.

The coverage issue also is difficult. Broad coverage can mean, as in the Boston State College contract, that the total structure of decision making in the institution is subject to bargaining and specified in the contract. This approach could result in a greatly diminished or even extinguished role for the academic senate. We prefer to this the current approach in Great Britain, where the bargaining association covers economic benefits and the faculty councils continue to treat academic affairs as entirely independent units, although we realize that this division of responsibilities is now being strongly challenged, and it may not be possible to retain it even in Great Britain. We believe, however, that this approach can better preserve faculty influence over academic matters once collective bargaining is undertaken. But it may be only a temporary solution. In any event, the contract should not provide for external arbitration over the granting of tenure except for determination of procedural disputes; the ultimate decisions about academic merit should be left in academic hands. Thus, *if* formal collective bargaining is to be undertaken at all, we favor a combination of codetermination for academic affairs and collective bargaining for economic matters, with the senate sharing certain managerial functions, and the union handling adversary functions.

Recommendation 18: The approach to contract coverage should be one of restraint, with the contract covering economic benefits and with academic affairs left (or put) in the hands of the faculty senate or equivalent council.

Much confusion now exists over bargaining units and contract coverage—some decisions have gone one way and others another way—and even over the right of faculty members to bargain at all in many states. Given the special nature of institutions of higher education—they are neither factories nor government departments—we favor special laws to cover bargaining by faculty members, or, if this is not possible, then special sections of laws or, at least, special administrative interpretations to reflect the special circumstances. The federal National Labor Relations Act is based on industrial experience. State laws on bargaining are based on the special nature of the civil service. The sharp industrial delineation between management and labor does not fit higher education; nor does the hierarchical civil service relation fit the more collegial approach taken on a campus. Faculty members are neither industrial workers nor civil servants. Their special profession and the special nature of the institution in which they are employed both call for separate treatment.

Recommendation 19: A separate federal law and separate state laws should be enacted governing collective bargaining by faculty members in both private and public institutions and should be responsive to the special circumstances that surround their employment. If this is not possible, then separate provisions should be made in more general laws, or leeway should be provided for special administrative interpretations.

Collective bargaining is new to higher education; it is also different from collective bargaining in other segments of society. Consequently, it would be most helpful if some centers or institutes could be established, or some existing ones extended in their interests, to collect contracts, review experience, and make information available to institutions of higher education across the country and to their faculties and to union organizations. We strongly encourage foundation and other financial support for these activities.

As we have noted earlier (Carnegie Commission, 1972b), institutions of higher education involved in collective bargaining will be well advised to employ experienced negotiators.

In any event, a period of unionization tends to be a difficult period as issues are developed and grievances sought out in the process of securing members for competing unions. The difficulties of this period should be anticipated.

Also, many different solutions will be found, reflecting, for example, the very great differences between and among the community colleges, the liberal arts colleges, the comprehensive colleges and universities, and the research universities. It is unlikely that any single standard pattern of relationships will emerge in the near future, if ever. A period of confusion and controversy should be expected.

Our general view is that collective bargaining, to the extent that it enters higher education, should not now become the new system of governance. Rather, it should be an amendment, in certain areas, to the existing forms of governance, as it has been, at least until now, in Great Britain. We believe this is the best current approach in the interests of preserving strong faculty influence over academic affairs, of assuring a heavy emphasis on quality and merit in making academic decisions, and of retaining a reasonable degree of independence from external control for institutions of higher education.

But history may carry higher education beyond its current state of development. We may be involved in a long-term period of greater social conflict in society and greater tension on campus. If so, it may be better to institutionalize this conflict through collective bargaining than to have it manifest itself with less restraint. Collective bargaining does provide agreed-upon rules of behavior, contractual understandings, and mechanisms for dispute settlement and grievance handling that help to manage conflict. Collective bargaining also provides a means through which the public interest in the conduct and the performance of the campus can be brought to bear upon decision making within the campus. Collective bargaining, thus, is one aspect of the rule of law, if and when a rule of law is required.

If consensus continues to disintegrate in academic life, then the codetermination that has accompanied it will be less effective, and collective bargaining will become more clearly preferable to an otherwise more anarchic situation. We have not clearly entered such a long-term period and we may not enter it, but we should recognize that aggravated conflict and collective bargaining may yet go hand in hand on campus in the future as greater consensus and codetermination have in the past.

7. Principles and Practices of Academic Tenure

Granting tenure is a long-established practice in most of the leading colleges and universities in the United States. It has gained in coverage and in strength particularly over the past half-century under the urging of the American Association of University Professors.[1] Virtually all universities and four-year colleges and over two-thirds of the two-year colleges have tenure practices. These practices vary substantially, with the variations reflecting, in part, the differing historical origins of tenure. One source has been the developing concept of academic freedom and tenure to protect it, particularly at first in leading research universities and then extended into other types of institutions; the other source has been seniority practices in the high schools that have been extended especially into the two-year colleges.

Hardly has the practice of tenure become well established, however, before it has met a widespread attack.

Many students now question tenure, charging that some faculty members are incompetent to teach and that many are too little concerned with teaching as compared with their other activities. Students interested in "student power" additionally recognize that a tenure contract places a most essential aspect of academic life outside of their short-term influence. Their opposition to tenure bears a resemblance to the opposition of the Jeffersonians to the Charter of Dartmouth College, which stood as a hand from the past controlling current events, and also placed them outside domination by public authority. A few students, furthermore, see tenure as a barrier against their wishes to politicize the faculty in accord with their own ideologies.

[1] See Appendix D for the association's policies on tenure.

Some members of the public at large, as in times past, attack tenure as an artificial protection for incompetent or politically unpopular professors. They argue that professors deserve no more security than anyone else, that they should not be a specially privileged class.

Some women and members of minority groups are increasingly doubtful about tenure practices, as expansion slows down, for fear that the practices may reduce their opportunities to move up the ladder, may foreclose their opportunities to replace male majority faculty members.

Tenure is now also more of a concern in the administration of a campus than in the past—for three main reasons.

First, the slowdown in new hiring, as the 1970s develop and as we move into the static enrollment of the 1980s, can mean a very high proportion of tenured faculty members. These faculty members will be older persons, and the opportunity to bring in younger scholars will decline, with a subsequent loss of new ideas and of vitality in the faculty. Given the heavy rate of hiring in the 1960s (about half of all current faculty members were employed in that decade), the "1960s faculty" will be the largest single seniority block in faculty councils until the year 2000, assuming that tenure protections are continued. We estimate that continuation of current trends will yield a nationwide full-time faculty in 1985 that is 80 percent tenured and 90 percent in 1990[2]—higher education will be substantially "tenured-in."

Second, student interests have become much more volatile with the changing labor market situation for college graduates and with the emergence of new social concerns (Peterson, 1972). A faculty predominantly tenured and committed to its historic specializations may find it hard to adjust the subject matter taught to the new interests of students.

Third, the "new depression" for higher education requires financial adjustments. About half of all the basic educational expenditures of a campus are related directly to the size of the faculty. Thus, a faculty with a high proportion of tenured members can introduce a rigidity into operations that makes financial savings more difficult.

The academic vitality of a faculty, its responsiveness to

[2] This assumes that faculty members will on the average receive tenure at the same age levels that they now do, and that average age will rise as new appointments decline in number.

changing student interests, and the degree of flexibility in its costs all relate to tenure under circumstances of a declining rate of increase in the number of new positions, a rising volatility in student choice of fields and subjects, and a continuing fiscal crisis.

Tenure, however, has several major advantages to the academic world and to society.

Tenure does add to the sense of academic freedom. Academic freedom should be and now largely is guaranteed to all faculty members, both with and without tenure, by institutional policies and by the actions of the American Association of University Professors; important aspects of it are also protected by the courts. The feeling of freedom, however, is undoubtedly somewhat increased by the tenure of professors who have it, not only because it gives them a sense of their own greater security but, perhaps even more, because their presence on the committees that hear cases that may arise about expressions of opinion gives a sense of protection to nontenured faculty.

Protection of academic freedom is important for faculty members, but it is even more important for the public as a whole. The public has a right to know what faculty members really think about scientific and scholarly issues, and it is in the public interest that they speak without fear of internal or external threat to their personal security. Society needs their free expression of opinion, within the law, for its own proper conduct and self-renewal.

Now that threats to freedom of expression come more frequently from within as well as from without the academic community, tenure has a doubled assignment in protecting academic freedom.

Tenure can and should protect the quality of a faculty. A decision as to whether a person receives tenure or not must be made, under model procedures, not later than the seventh year of his or her employment. This time for decision can and should give rise to the most careful review of past performance and future potential. In the absence of such a review point, there is a tendency to postpone difficult decisions year by year until time itself makes the decision. An alternative to tenure is some sort of a seniority system that probably would never give as great security as tenure does, but starts its protection much earlier (perhaps after the first or second year) and does not provide for such a searching review at any point. It takes a long time for a faculty member to demonstrate competence in all the usual areas under review—teaching, research, campus service, and public service. A long probationary period and careful review at its conclusion are essential to the quality of a faculty. Tenure rules provide for such a period and such review.

Additionally, faculty members are participants in the governance of the academic enterprise. It helps to have some of them denoted as "full partners"—as in a law firm—with a responsibility for the long-run welfare of the institution and the careful selection of their junior colleagues, a concern for the maintenance and improvement of the collections in the library, and a willingness to do overhead work like serving on committees and in administrative capacities—as for example, do department chairmen. Tenure is one way of attracting valued faculty members to an institution—Eliot changed and strengthened it at Harvard for just this purpose—and they, in turn, have a greater interest in such endeavors as alumni relations and public representation. Tenure is a mechanism for providing responsible leadership and continuity in a faculty.

Greater assurance of academic freedom for faculty members to express unpopular opinions, greater protection for the public in its access to the full and free views of faculty members, greater opportunity for a more serious review of the quality of faculty members, and a fuller feeling of partnership in the campus enterprise by senior faculty members are the basic reasons for tenure. They are, we believe, quite persuasive. This does not mean, however, that the principle of tenure has not on occasion been improperly applied in practice and that it need not be freed of its abuses in the future.

To make tenure both more effective in achieving its positive benefits and to avoid its deterioration through abuses, we believe that in all institutions:

- Appointments and promotions to tenure should be made only after the most careful review. One test of the care of this review is how many persons eligible for tenure are not given tenure. If tenure is automatic, then tenure serves much less of a purpose and may serve none at all. Boards of trustees should receive an annual report on the number of eligible persons granted and not granted tenure. Another test is the proportion of tenure appointments to persons from outside as compared to persons from inside the campus. There should be no instant or automatic tenure for those already on the job. In a majority of two-year colleges in a recent year (1971), however, 100 percent of all persons considered for tenure actually received tenure (Furniss, 1972).

- "Merit" increases after tenure should be on the basis of merit and not seniority, otherwise a reward for good performance is removed and a penalty for poor performance is forgone. The percentage of persons given merit increases, as compared with those eligible, is an indication of how much merit there is in merit increases. The board of trustees should also have an annual report on these percentages.

- A "Bill of Rights and Responsibilities" (Carnegie Commission, 1971 *b*), at least in large institutions, should guide the conduct of faculty members.

- A statement of "Rights of Students to Receive Instruction" (Carnegie Commission, 1972*a*) can help protect students from abuses growing out of faculty neglect of duty.

- A broader interpretation than has been customary should be made of the requirements of institutional welfare as a basis for ceasing the employment of tenured faculty members. Financial insolvency or total abandonment of a field should not alone justify termination. The needs of institutional welfare should allow cessation of employment also for such causes as (1) substantial and continued reduction of student interest in a field, and (2) consolidation of work in a field, within a multicampus system or within a consortium, on a single campus or on a smaller number of campuses. It should also be possible, and may often be desirable from the point of view of the individual faculty member, to make reasonable reassignments outside of the specific field and location of the original assignment at the time when tenure was granted.

- So that fully impartial decisions may be made about terminations of tenured faculty members or other adverse actions taken against them for "cause" or for the sake of institutional welfare, it is essential that clear and reasonable rules be in force and that independent tribunals including persons from outside the school, college, or campus of the individual potentially affected, be available (Carnegie Commission, 1971*b*). Any profession is hesitant to penalize its own members. This hesitancy is heightened if the member in question is also a close friend or colleague of persons serving on the judicial tribunal. Separate procedures may be desirable for "economic" cases (reduction of staff) as compared with "freedom" cases. The former might be placed before a "budget" committee and the latter before a "privilege and tenure" committee.

- Some reasonable percentage needs to be set well in advance to indicate a "peril point" where the percentage of tenured faculty members may be deemed excessive. The current actual figure of faculty members with tenure across the United States is 49 percent (Appendix A, Table A-19). Institutions already above the 50 percent figure, in particular, should consider their future policies. Since 1939, Harvard has had a carefully worked out formula governing the number of tenured faculty members in each department. Very few other institutions now have any limitations at all (Furniss, 1972). The purpose of this suggested concern for the percentage of faculty members with tenure is to preserve opportunities for new additions to the staff, including women and members of minority groups, and for adjustments to changing student interests and to financial pressures. We are concerned particularly that proper consideration be given to persons in the "external market" as well as to those already in the "internal market," that those already inside do not unduly monopolize opportunities to the detriment of those presently outside or who in the future will stand outside trying to move inside.

Provided these policies and practices are in effect, it is our conviction that the principle of tenure has clear advantages both for academic institutions and for American society. Any such revisions in tenure practices, however, will meet with substantial resistance, particularly now that there are fewer places for faculty members to go once they have ceased to be employed by an institution, now that unionization is spreading, and now that courts are hearing more cases and setting more precise standards for review procedures.

Recommendation 20: The principle of tenure should be retained and extended to campuses where it does not now apply.

Recommendation 21: Tenure systems should be so administered in practice (1) that advancements to tenure and after tenure are based on merit, (2) that the criteria to be used in tenure decisions are made clear at the time of employment, (3) that codes of conduct specify the obligations of tenured faculty members, (4) that adjustments in the size and in the assignments of staff in accord with institutional welfare be possible when there is a fully justifiable case for them, (5) that fair internal procedures be available to hear any cases that may arise, and (6) that the percentage of faculty members with tenure does not become excessive.

Persons on a part-time basis have a particularly difficult time accumulating a record that merits tenure over the same elapsed period (essentially six years) as for full-time persons. Consequently it would seem reasonable that, where such persons are on a 50-percent time basis or more, they should be eligible for tenure, but that the amount of time to earn tenure should be calculated on a full-time-equivalent basis and not on calendar years served.

Recommendation 22: Persons on a 50-percent time basis or more should be eligible for tenure, but the time elapsed before a decision on tenure must be made should be counted on a full-time-equivalent basis.

More and more persons denied tenure are protesting the decision. Denial of tenure, however, is not the same as dismissal. Persons denied tenure, nevertheless, should be given the reasons if they request them and should be able to ask for reconsideration. But, if they do so, the burden of proof should be on them and no appeal on other than procedural questions should be possible outside the traditional academic authority of faculty committees, president, and trustees. We do not believe that external arbitrators should be able to grant tenure, and we believe that courts both do and should respect academic judgments fairly arrived at. If unfair procedures, however, are found to have resulted in denial of tenure, then the decision should be reconsidered by the appropriate academic authority. Granting tenure is ultimately a decision that should be made on the basis of academic judgments alone. The granting of tenure should be viewed as a positive act based on meritorious achievement—essentially as a new decision, and not as a reversal of a prior decision to employ. The bases upon which tenure decisions will be judged should be made available in writing at the time of employment to nontenured faculty members.

Term contracts, for example for six years, are now being suggested as an alternative to tenure and are occasionally adopted. We oppose this solution, except under exceptional circumstances, for these reasons: (1) academic review will be less thorough if another review is possible six years hence—the tendency in borderline cases will be to avoid a negative decision; (2) after 12 years, it is unlikely that a person will be dropped in any event; and (3) persons with contracts will vote on each other's contracts—under tenure only faculty members with tenure vote on persons without tenure—and the process of voting on each other's contracts can be personally awkward and creates possibilities of either positive mutual courtesies or negative factional retribution.

A special review at age 60, in addition to the normal periodic "merit" review, provided a generous retirement plan is in operation, warrants careful consideration.

Tenure, in its derivation from land tenure, means not the ownership of a position but the right to hold it under certain conditions. Ownership implies the right to use, or not to use, or even to misuse. Tenure implies the right to make *good* use. It is the definition of "good use" that warrants reconsideration, not the concept of tenure itself.

In general, we endorse the principle of academic tenure but believe that changes should be made in some of the policies and practices that now accompany it.

8. Student Influence on Campus and off

Students in the early Colonial period had little freedom or influence and no power. There was a single curriculum, and there were rigid rules of conduct enforced by faculty proctors. A long struggle against the fixed curriculum and against *in loco parentis* ensued which is, by now, largely won. Beginning around the Civil War, elective courses were introduced that gave more options to students and increased their influence through their choices of courses and professors. Then, particularly after the Civil War and through the 1920s, students developed their own extracurricular activities—athletic teams, literary magazines, newspapers, theatrical societies, debating teams. In more recent times, a new period has begun. Students have taken more of an interest in political activity off campus and some have sought to use the campus as a base for such activity. Some have also taken more of an interest in academic and administrative developments in addition to extracurricular activities on campus. Students have gone outside the walls of the campus into the surrounding society and also have sought to enter the inner sanctum of academic and administrative policies long reserved for faculty members, administrators, and trustees.

This new move forward in the long-term historical development of greater student freedom and influence within higher education has followed a massive increase in student numbers, a greater average size of campus, an energizing of students through their concerns about domestic and foreign affairs, and the advent of TV, through which students, like other groups, can present their cases most dramatically to the public.

Additionally, the 18-year-old vote now gives students potential influence in state capitols and Congressional halls beyond anything known before, and often beyond the influence students have on campus over their own faculty senates and boards of trustees. For the first time, undergraduate students can potentially bring authoritative outside pressure to bear on faculties and trustees—their external power may come to exceed their internal influence. The best way to reach the administration in Bascom Hall at Madison may come to be to go down State Street to the capitol building and then come back up the street to Bascom Hall. This new road to power draws on the greater potential responsiveness of legislators than of faculty members to students—legislators may be inherently more sympathetic to student desires than are faculty members, and they may also have less to lose personally by supporting students in some of their campus-centered demands. Potentially, they have something to gain in votes at election time.

The political calculus favors the students more in the legislative halls than in the faculty councils. This fact of life can shift the balance of power on campus as students seek external solutions to internal conflicts of interest. Faculty members will welcome student assistance in obtaining higher salaries from the legislature but will regret any legislative intrusion into academic affairs. Students, in turn, in contact with political reality and public opinion, may tend to become more realistic and sophisticated about goals and tactics. This development of external political power by students, however, poses problems for the autonomy of the campus. The legislature, for one more reason, may take over more of the traditional authority of the board of trustees.

Dissent against society and participation within the academic affairs of the campus are the new manifestations of the intermittent three-century-old drive of students for a position of greater influence, and use of TV and political lobbying are among the new tactics. This drive seems, at the moment, to be in low gear. We do not believe, however, that this signals an end to all further attempts at forward motion. We believe, rather, that the long-run student concern for greater influence, while rising and falling in intensity of expression, will continue into the indefinite future. The problems of the recent past with student demands for power have not disappeared forever. They need to be faced either now or later. It is our conviction that it is better to examine them now, in a period that allows careful consideration, than it is to postpone examination until some later date when sober reflection may be more of a luxury.

Higher education has moved into the 1970s with students on most campuses having achieved increased influence in areas of decision making. Data from the Carnegie Commission survey of 1969–70 indicated, however, that students are divided among themselves about the extent of influence they should have. Only a very few students then wanted control over academic decisions; many wanted more power through voting roles on committees; most believed they should be consulted, either formally or informally. (See Charts 2 and 3 and Appendix A, Tables A-20 through A-32.) On many campuses, student power is, of course, less of an active issue now than it was in 1969–70. Student attitudes as expressed in 1969–70 may be summarized as follows:

- Both undergraduate and graduate student interests in participation are expressed in declining order in the following areas: (1) student discipline, (2) provision and content of courses, (3) degree requirements, (4) admissions policies, (5) faculty appointments and promotions. For undergraduates, residence hall regulations have highest ranking.

- Similar proportions of graduate students and undergraduates desire voting power on committees dealing with academic issues. A majority of each group, however, favors less than such a voting rule.

- On the issue of the provision and content of courses, at least formal consultation is desired by 77 percent of undergraduates and 79 percent of graduate students; at least a voting role on committees by 43 percent of undergraduates and 42 percent of graduate students; and control by 4 percent of undergraduates and 4 percent of graduate students.

- Graduate student attitudes toward the decision-making role of undergraduates are more like those of faculty members than like those of undergraduates.

- Students in the social sciences, humanities, law, and education/social welfare generally are most desirous of greater influence, and those in engineering and other professions (except health and law) are least desirous.

- While differences among fields are greater than differences among types of institutions, students in the more academically prestigious liberal arts colleges are generally most desirous of greater influence, and those in the two-year colleges least desirous.

Faculty members are generally much more reluctant about a decision-making role for students than are the students. Faculty

CHART 2 *Faculty and undergraduate student attitudes about undergraduate student participation*

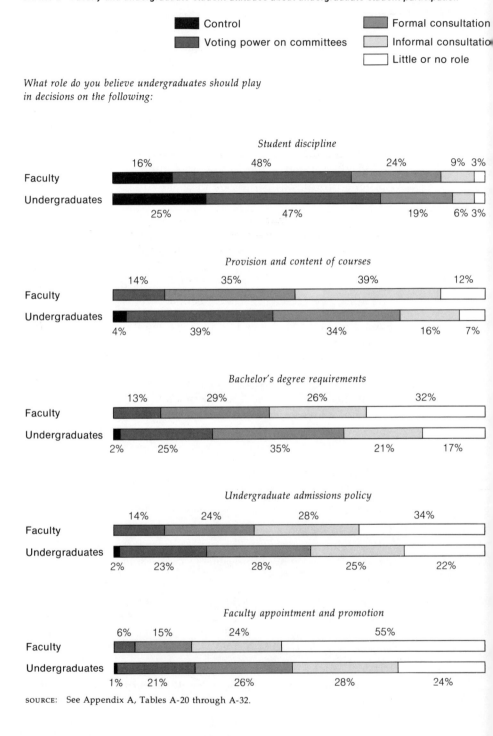

■ Control   ■ Formal consultation

■ Voting power on committees   ▨ Informal consultation

☐ Little or no role

*What role do you believe undergraduates should play
in decisions on the following:*

Student discipline

Faculty: 16% | 48% | 24% | 9% | 3%

Undergraduates: 25% | 47% | 19% | 6% | 3%

Provision and content of courses

Faculty: 14% | 35% | 39% | 12%

Undergraduates: 4% | 39% | 34% | 16% | 7%

Bachelor's degree requirements

Faculty: 13% | 29% | 26% | 32%

Undergraduates: 2% | 25% | 35% | 21% | 17%

Undergraduate admissions policy

Faculty: 14% | 24% | 28% | 34%

Undergraduates: 2% | 23% | 28% | 25% | 22%

Faculty appointment and promotion

Faculty: 6% | 15% | 24% | 55%

Undergraduates: 1% | 21% | 26% | 28% | 24%

SOURCE: See Appendix A, Tables A-20 through A-32.

CHART 3 *Faculty and graduate student attitudes about graduate student participation*

■ Control   ▦ Formal consultation

▦ Voting power on committees   ▦ Informal consultation

☐ Little or no role

*What role do you believe graduate students should play
in decisions on the following:*

Student discipline

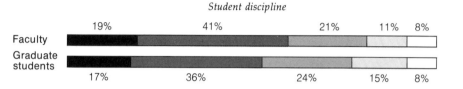

Provision and content of graduate courses

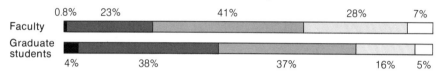

Advanced degree requirements

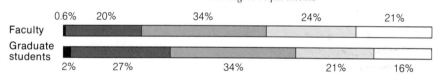

Departmental graduate admissions policy

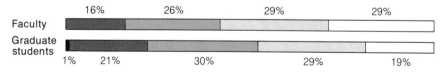

Faculty appointment and promotion

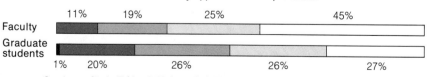

SOURCE: See Appendix A, Tables A-20 through A-32.

attitudes (see Charts 1 and 2, and Appendix A, Tables A-20 through A-32) may be summarized as follows:

- Only one area exists where a majority of faculty members are willing to turn over at least "voting power" to both undergraduate and graduate students, and that is the area of student discipline. Faculty members historically have not liked the disciplinary role. Faculty members are most overwhelmingly opposed to student "control" or "voting power" in connection with faculty appointments and promotions. A majority say students should have "little or no role" in this area.

- Faculty members are generally more willing to share influence over academic matters with graduate students than with undergraduates, particularly over the provision and content of courses and degree requirements.

- While few faculty are willing to grant "voting power" to students, large proportions say students should be formally consulted. Faculty support for at least "formal consultation" is expressed in the same ordering of issue areas as that given by students. Faculty support is greater in those fields and types of institutions where student interests also are greatest—highest in the liberal arts colleges and lowest in the community colleges.

- In the area of provision and content of courses, nearly two-thirds (65 percent) of faculty members are willing to consult formally with graduate students, and almost half (49 percent) with undergraduates. A majority of faculty in the social sciences, humanities, law, health, and education would grant such influence to undergraduates.

- Younger faculty members are generally more willing to share influence with students than are older faculty members, but even they are unwilling to share "control" or "voting power" with undergraduate or graduate students except in the area of student discipline.

- Faculty members in departments that have granted graduate students substantial influence are generally more favorable to graduate student influence than are those in departments that have not done so. This implies that the faculty members were more inclined to do so to begin with—otherwise they probably would not have granted the influence—but it also implies that the experience has, at least, not been sufficiently unfavorable so as to change their attitudes, and it may even have made them more favorable.

- A majority of faculty members (55 percent) "strongly agree" or "agree with reservations" that student evaluations of their teachers should play a part in faculty promotions.

Political leaning is generally related to attitudes about student participation, with attitudes of those students and faculty members who classify themselves as politically "left" being quite divergent. Among them the emphasis on "participatory democracy" is comparatively very high. A wide gap exists between members of this group and all other students and faculty members. (See Appendix A, Tables A-30 through A-32). The size of this "left" group is about 5 percent of the total for both students and faculty members. It is somewhat higher than this in the more academically prestigious liberal arts colleges and in the leading research universities. (See Appendix A, Table A-1.) The "left" faculty members, aside from political conviction, may also be searching for allies among the students. The faculty generally, however, regardless of how liberal it may be off campus about power relationships, is clearly conservative on campus about its own power.

Recent alumni, most interestingly, have the same hierarchy of areas as the students in which they believe students should have greater influence. Alumni support student participation in decisions about rules and curriculum more than they do about admission standards or faculty tenure appointments (Spaeth & Greeley, 1970).

We conclude from this and other evidence that:

- Very few students want to "take over" academic life and control it.

- Most students, however, want a better chance to participate in decision making about academic life either through voting rights, or formal or informal consultation.

- Little common cause exists between faculty members and students in academic governance (except in the area of discipline). Students generally want more authority than faculty members are prepared to concede, with the exception of the 5 percent of faculty members who are "left." This gap between faculty and students is largely a new one, for students have never before so sought to enter areas occupied by faculty authority.

- Many faculty members, however, are willing to consult formally about courses and about degree requirements, particularly at the graduate level.

- Faculty members are also prepared to have students evaluate their teaching performance.

- Student interests and faculty willingness are high in the same subject-matter fields and the same types of institutions; and faculty and student support for participation is the same with respect to the ordering of issue areas—the rankings correspond but at a substantially lower level of support among faculty members.

The Carnegie Commission is generally sympathetic to greater student participation in those areas of governance where they have substantial interest and adequate competence, and where they will assume responsibility. We believe that in such areas students can inform the decision-making agencies about their experiences and desires, give good advice, exercise good judgment, and support innovation. We also strongly emphasize the educational value of participation in governance. We recognize, at the same time, that there are difficulties: How many students will involve themselves in governance? Will students attend committee meetings regularly? Will they inform themselves adequately and take responsibility? Can they be effective or accountable in the absence of well-defined constituencies and continuity of membership?

We believe that governance can be improved to the extent that:

- Students are given reasonable academic options—in choice of curricula and courses and in stopping-in and stopping-out—from among which they may choose.

- Hearings are held on topics of general campus concern where students may make presentations.

- Students either serve on joint committees along with faculty members and/or trustees or administrators and have voting rights in areas of their interest and competence, or have their own parallel committees that meet with faculty and/or trustee or administrative committees.[1] We suggest such opportunities in connection with committees such as those on courses, educational policy, student affairs, public lectures and events, libraries, degree requirements, admissions policies, and student discipline. In the case of student discipline, the administration generally has both more interest and more responsibility than does the faculty and should be adequately represented depending on the nature of the case. We do not favor having students serve on boards of trustees or in faculty senates or in departments. We favor instead students

[1] For a discussion of the comparative values of consultation versus voting rights see Shils (1970); and Ashby and Anderson (1971).

having voting rights on selected committees or rights of formal consultation in selected areas at each of these levels.

▪ Students who serve on joint or parallel committees with major responsibilities are given staff assistance so that they may be better informed
and can reduce the amount of time it takes to be effective members.
They should have access to the same information as all other committee members. A record of their service should be made a part of their
college transcript, if they request it.

▪ Students evaluate the teaching performance of faculty members and
this evaluation is made a part of the record when promotions are considered. We do not favor students serving on appointment and promotion committees (Carnegie Commission, 1972*a*).

▪ Student governments have substantial authority over student activities; and student cooperatives are encouraged in such areas as book-
stores, residences, and eating facilities.

▪ Codes of conduct are developed, after consultation with and participation by students, setting forth the general rights and responsibilities of
members of the campus community and, more specifically, the rights
of students to receive instruction under favorable circumstances (Carnegie Commission, 1971*b*, 1972*a*).

▪ The campus has an ombudsman or equivalent, adequate formal grievance machinery, and provision for appeals to impartial judicial tribunals.

Some of the most valuable contributions of student participation can be at the departmental level, which is the most active
working level of the campus. Students are often a large and het-
erogeneous group, but within their major fields they are less
numerous and more homogeneous. Student representatives on
departmental advisory committees (or on parallel committees)
can encourage participation by other students by holding open
hearings on proposals under discussion in committee, and by
circulating written information and opinion questionnaires.
Like any other committee member, the student representative's
final vote or recommendation should reflect his own best judgments. When a recommendation of a faculty-student committee
(or a parallel committee) is brought before the departmental faculty, student committee members should have the right to attend the meeting to present their views if they wish to do so.
(For an excellent discussion of student participation, see Appendix E.)

The processes of selecting student members of joint committees or parallel committees is an important issue. We favor their selection at the departmental level (or at the course level in large departments): (1) students at this level are more likely to meet face-to-face and to know each other. This makes the selection process more informed and makes it easier for the person chosen to consult with other students and to report back; and (2) great variation exists in student experiences and interests among departments (English literature versus engineering, for example) and thus representation chosen at this level will bring in a greater variety of opinion, opinion that is related to actual operating situations. It is important, in any event, to specify the definition of the electorate and the processes of selection. For committees above the departmental level, we suggest that departmental representation be formed into an electoral body to select members.

We wish to caution against hasty consideration of "community councils" or "universitywide senates," whether of the advisory type such as at Princeton or the legislative type such as at New Hampshire. Several experiments are now going on (see Appendix C) and they should be studied carefully. The experience to date indicates quite mixed results. Such councils may add to the solution of problems or they may detract from solutions, depending on the situation. Their impact on the academic authority of faculty senates and/or faculty departments, the "trust" authority of trustees, and the politicalization of issues on campus needs careful consideration. Where such councils are created, we believe that it is best that they have advisory authority only. On an advisory basis they can be, and often have been, most helpful not only for the sake of consultation on emergency situations but also as a means of airing and exploring continuing problems, attitudes, and relationships. Many issues are of concern to several of the constituencies on a campus, and great benefit can result from the joint discussion of them preparatory to decision by the authorities with power to act. But careful attention needs to be given to the means of selecting members.

We also wish to caution against improper use of external influence by student "lobbies." A few already have substantial influence because of the persuasive abilities of their representatives and their prospective impact on the 18- to 21-year-old vote. This influence can be used to secure, through legislation, concessions that students may not be able to obtain internally. Sometimes this may be both necessary and desirable, but at other times it may intrude upon the long-term independence of the institution. To the extent that these lobbies obtain power, they will need to exercise restraint in its use. Given such restraint, they can be a constructive force.

We suggest that in some situations it may be desirable if students (and also faculty members, separately or together with students) are given the opportunity to nominate a certain number of trustees, as alumni now often do, or otherwise to join in the nomination process. Any persons so nominated should be drawn from persons external to the campus so that conflicts of interest are avoided. There has been a long-time practice in the Scottish universities for students to elect one or more outside persons as members of governing bodies.

Recommendation 23: Governance arrangements should provide: (1) adequate academic options from among which students may choose, and (2) the right to be heard on important campus issues.

Recommendation 24: Students should serve on joint faculty-student (or trustee-student or administrative-student) committees with the right to vote or should have their own parallel student committees with the right to meet with faculty, trustee, and administrative committees in areas of special interest and competence such as educational policy and student affairs. Students serving on such committees should be given staff assistance.

Recommendation 25: Students should be given the opportunity to evaluate the teaching performance of faculty members, and students should be involved in periodic reviews of the performance of departments (Carnegie Commission, 1972*a*).

Recommendation 26: Conduct codes should be prepared with student involvement in the process of their preparation, ombudsmen or their equivalent should be appointed, and formal grievance machinery should be available and should end in impartial judicial tribunals.

We believe that majority student wishes (as expressed in the 1969–70 survey) for more participation can generally be accommodated within the governance arrangements of colleges and universities while adding to the information available and to the quality of the judgments exercised in making decisions. Another step forward is now being taken in the historic process of giving students more freedom and influence without impeding—and perhaps enhancing—the quality of academic life. Students should be involved in governance to the extent—which in some areas can be significant—that they contribute to the quality of decisions and to the overall performance of the campus, and not on the basis of disruptive tactics. Students should now be incorporated more fully into the on going decision-making processes on campus within the limits of their interest, their competence, and their ability to take responsibility.

9. Emergency or Unprogrammed Decision Making

The academic world traditionally has been one of continuity in institutional structures and processes—"nothing should ever be done for the first time" (Cornford, 1953, p. 15)—with few sharp breaks in the pattern of gradual change. Decisions have been made slowly, after consultation, or not made at all if any major opposition has been expressed. The strategy has been to build consensus, to avoid conflict among colleagues. Decision making has been shared by boards, presidents, and faculties, with little provision for participation by students or by external groups.

Suddenly the situation changed in the 1960s. Quick actions became more necessary. New groups were now knocking on the doors to be let into the corridors of power. New tactics were used—not only the old normal channels of discussion but also the new "normal channels of confrontation." Some decisions could no longer wait for the slow formation of consensus, nor could they be made within the confines of the councils composed only of the old proprietors of power.

Many new stresses have developed on campus; many new strains have been introduced into the groves of academe; many mistakes have been made. The old mechanisms of governance have often not been equal to the new situation. The academic world had done quite well in governing itself within the less tumultuous conditions of the past, and it has proved its ability to handle programmed decisions about slowly developing problems. The new context, however, is more dynamic, and more of the decisions now have to be handled on an unprogrammed basis—quicker responses are needed and are undertaken in a more complex setting. More individuals and groups are involved.

Much of the sense of urgency of the late 1960s has subsided, it is true, but not all of it, and circumstances may serve to increase it again in the future.

We have earlier set forth our views on how to be prepared for contingencies (Carnegie Commission, 1971*b*). In summary they are:

- The need for a formal Bill of Rights and Responsibilities of the members of the campus, so that the basic rules may be known in advance

- The need for the clearest possible distinction between dissent and disruption, with full protection for the former and full opposition to the latter

- The need for good consultative machinery quickly available, for quick and accurate means of communication, and for clear lines of authority understood in advance

- The advisability of advance consultation with law enforcement agencies and of good channels of communication with them

- The desirability for adequate grievance machinery, including impartial judicial boards in the "hard" cases, such as those involving political protest

Generally we endorsed the report of the President's Commission on Campus Unrest (Scranton Commission). We repeat this endorsement and reaffirm the recommendations in our own prior report.

10. Governance—Return to Consensus or Adjustment to Conflict?

Governance of higher education in the United States has never experienced an entirely problem-free Golden Age to which an easy return might be made. Nostalgia aside, there always have been some troubles. However, one recent period, roughly the two decades after World War II, was marked by at least a surface consensus about what was good practice. This apparent consensus may have rested on top of many suppressed antagonisms, or on mere acceptance of what seemed inevitable and unchangeable, or on just a deep layer of apathy. But there was a substantial amount of acceptance—much of it we believe was quite wholehearted—about how things should be done:

- Governors and legislators should be "quick to help and slow to interfere," as Daniel Coit Gilman once expressed it.
- Boards of trustees should watch out for the money, care for the grounds and buildings, and appoint a good president.
- The president should raise money, ward off external attacks and be a good friend of faculty, students, and alumni.
- Faculty members should make academic decisions through their departments and their senate committees subject only to occasional veto on good grounds. Their right to tenure was usually taken for granted.
- Students should run their extracurricula activities and stay out of academic decisions.
- Decisions should be made with due deliberation; there were few crises and fewer confrontations.

As we have seen above, several of these points of consensus have been challenged in recent years. Conflict over governance has intensified on campus, and between the campus and society. There has been for a long time, of course, much debate on campus about intellectual matters, and between the campus and some elements of society over the views of some faculty members—the campus has not been a place of total harmony internally or externally—but we are concerned here only with acceptance of, or disagreement about, modes of governance, and there once was more acceptance and less disagreement than now exists.

The old consensus may again be restored—and the immediate period (1973) is one of comparative calm that may mark a return to the older consensus, but it may instead be only a time of reaction after a period of turmoil, a temporary lull. We believe that it is unlikely that the old consensus will suffice for the future. A new situation exists both in the relation of the campus to society and on the campus itself:

- American society is going through a period of social transformation, and the campus is more a part of society than ever before. The campus is also more a center for social conflict than it once was—it may even be taking the place once held by the farm when rural populism was a great force, and by the factory when organized labor was rising to a position of new power. The campus is intimately involved in cultural change.

- Intellectuals, with their principal base on campus, are often in substantial conflict with their surrounding societies in each of the advanced industrial nations, including the United States. They are more active in political life. New styles of life are being born on campus in an age when the cultural model of society is subject to challenge.

- Higher education itself is moving from the stage of mass access to one of universal access. This increases public interest in it. Also, new knowledge and new ideas are more important to society, and their main source is now on campus. Also, the leadership of society is now more largely selected and trained on campus; the new meritocratic elite is first identified there.

- The campus is more of a source of change in society and less an element of stability; thus it is a more controversial element of society. It is more of a force in society.

- Public authority is being extended over many aspects of American society, including, and perhaps particularly, the campus because of its now more central role.

- Faculty members are more divided than before between adherence to objectivity versus adherence to social commitment; they are more divided over the appropriate forms of campus governance.

- Students have been energized by the problems of society to take a greater interest in the conduct of society and in the conduct of the campus as a focal institution in society. A new gap has emerged between many of them and many faculty members over student participation in academic decision making.

- Authority on campus has been more subject to challenge—particularly the authority of the trustees and the president.

As a consequence of these and other forces at work, higher education must contemplate the possibility that greater conflict over governance will characterize the future than it did the earlier post-World War II period. Conflict within the campus and between the campus and society over the location of power may be more than a passing phase identified with the special problems of the late 1960s. If so, governance will be a continuing source of concern.

We hope that a new consensus over governance can be achieved, and our suggestions above are set forth in the hope that:

- Understandings may be reached between public authorities and higher education over campus independence

- The essential roles of the board of trustees and the president may be accepted, and that boards may be better constituted to carry out their roles

- The codetermination rights of faculty members in areas of academic decision making may be extended where they do not now prevail and may be preserved where they do

- The principle of tenure may be retained, although its practice should be subject to review

- The views of students, on a regularized basis, may be better incorporated into decision-making processes

- Better rules may be developed setting forth the rights and responsibilities of members of the academic community, and better mechanisms may be developed to govern conflict and to adjudicate disputes

A consensus over governance depends, in part, on a consensus about purposes. Rules governing independence, for example, are not so important when there is general agreement between society and the campus about purposes as when there is disagreement. The location of authority on campus, as another example, is not so crucial an issue when there is agreement about purposes as when there is not. Firmness of purposes is a strong foundation for governance; weakness has its costs. Thus what happens to governance depends heavily on what happens about purposes.

The suggestions we have made above are set forth as the possible basis for a new consensus about governance. Should no new consensus be developed, we believe, nevertheless, that the policies we have recommended above should be followed. In fact, they may be even more important as bases for living with conflict. But, in the absence of consensus, the rules will become more detailed and precise, the mechanisms more formalized and burdensome, the hand of authority more evident and heavier, and the tone of relationships will also become much harsher and more unpleasant. Shared understandings, mutual goodwill, and fewer rules are much preferable. One of the best signs of a striferidden set of relationships is a thick, and thickening, book of rules.

The spirit of the enterprise is at stake. A major effort should be made to seek a new consensus as a first order of priority.

Should conflict continue, however, it will then need to be institutionalized within more specific rules, will need to be adjudicated by more effective mechanisms, will need to be guided in constructive directions. And this may be the new—and more difficult—role of governance: to manage conflict rather than to preside over consensus or apathy or resignation masquerading as consensus, to defend institutional independence in the absence of broad societal approval, to arbitrate internal disputes in the absence of tolerance and goodwill. If this should be the course of future events for campus governance, then higher education will have followed other elements of society that have preceded it into the mainstream of social tensions. The campus will then have to prepare itself to turn temporarily unsolvable issues and irreconcilable principles and intense personal conflicts into the most peaceful and rational processes possible of internal decision making.

The suggestions we have made above are set forth as the possible basis for a new consensus about governance.

Failures of structures and processes of governance did not basically cause the problems of recent years; and better structures and processes will not, by themselves, overcome current problems—but they may alleviate their negative impacts; and worse structures and processes may, of course, equally aggravate them.

The basic test of governance, as we see it, is whether the decisions actually made do or do not enhance the long-run welfare of higher education and of society, and the quality of the individual campus, and whether the solutions are appropriate to and commensurate with the problems. A second test is whether the processes followed gain respect and a sense of legitimacy and trust—"government by consent and after consultation" (Ashby, 1966, p. 108). To this end we have sought in our recommendations to assure that all who have a substantial interest in a decision may have their views heard about it, and that all who have competence to make the decision, and who must take responsibility for it, have a chance, directly or through their representatives, to participate in making the decision. Both the products and the processes of decision making are subject to evaluation.

In conclusion, acknowledging the importance of structures and processes and the need for their improvement, we note that the quality of governance depends in the end, and above all else, on the people who participate in it.

References

Ashby, Eric: *Technology and the Academics,* Macmillan, London, 1966.

Ashby, Eric, and Mary Anderson: "Consultation or Voting Power," *Minerva,* vol. 9, pp. 400–405, July 1971.

Boyd, William B.: "The Impact of Collective Bargaining on University Governance," *Liberal Education,* vol. 58, pp. 265–271, May 1972.

Carnegie Commission on Higher Education: "National Survey of Higher Education," directed by Martin Trow, Berkeley, Calif., 1969. Unpublished.

Carnegie Commission on Higher Education: *Less Time, More Options: Education Beyond the High School,* McGraw-Hill Book Company, New York, 1970a.

Carnegie Commission on Higher Education: *A Chance to Learn: An Action Agenda for Equal Opportunity in Higher Education,* McGraw-Hill Book Company, New York, 1970b.

Carnegie Commission on Higher Education: *New Students and New Places: Policies for the Future Growth and Development of American Higher Education,* McGraw-Hill Book Company, New York, 1971a.

Carnegie Commission on Higher Education: *Dissent and Disruption: Proposals for Consideration by the Campus,* McGraw-Hill Book Company, New York, 1971b.

Carnegie Commission on Higher Education: *The Capitol and the Campus: State Responsibility for Postsecondary Education,* McGraw-Hill Book Company, New York, 1971c.

Carnegie Commission on Higher Education: *Reform on Campus: Changing Students, Changing Academic Programs,* McGraw-Hill Book Company, New York, 1972a.

Carnegie Commission on Higher Education: *The More Effective Use of Resources: An Imperative for Higher Education,* McGraw-Hill Book Company, New York, 1972b.

Cornford, F. M.: *Microcosmographia Academia,* Bowes and Bowes, Cambridge, 1953.

Furniss, W. Todd: "Faculty Tenure and Contract Systems: Current Practice," American Council on Education, special report, Washington, D.C., July 27, 1972.

Garbarino, Joseph W.: "Creeping Unionism and the Faculty Labor Market," in Margaret S. Gordon (ed.), *Higher Education and the Labor Market,* McGraw-Hill Book Company, New York, forthcoming.

Gross, Edward, and Paul V. Grambsch: *Change in University Organization, 1964–1971,* McGraw-Hill Book Company, New York, forthcoming.

Lee, Eugene C. and Frank M. Bowen: *The Multicampus University: A Study of Academic Governance,* McGraw-Hill Book Company, New York, 1971.

Peterson, Richard E.: *American College and University Enrollment Trends in 1971,* Carnegie Commission on Higher Education, Berkeley, Calif., 1972.

Shils, Edward: "Student Participation: Consultation or Voting Power," *Minerva,* vol. 8, pp. 611–623, October 1970.

Spaeth, Joe L., and Andrew M. Greeley: *Recent Alumni and Higher Education,* McGraw-Hill Book Company, New York, 1970.

Appendix A: Tables from the Carnegie Commission Surveys on Student and Faculty Attitudes

The tables in this appendix are based on the Carnegie Commission mailed surveys conducted in 1969. Undergraduates were sampled in 189 institutions, graduate students in 158, and faculty in 303 institutions. Questionnaires were answered by 70,772 undergraduates, 32,963 graduate students, and 60,028 faculty members. For economy in data processing, random subsamples were selected from each of these three large samples, and much of the data presented in this report are based on these subsamples. The unweighted number of cases in the samples are: undergraduates, 10,002, graduate students, 8,500, faculty members, 8,500. Most data in Tables A.2 through A.14, and the data in A-19 are based on the full faculty sample of 60,028 respondents.

All data have been weighted to compensate for differential rates of sampling among institutions of different types and qualities, and for differential rates of response among institutions.

Detailed information on these surveys can be found in Martin Trow, et al., *National Surveys of Higher Education*, Berkeley, Calif., 1971.

For a description of the Carnegie Commission classification of institutions, see Appendix B of this report.

List of Tables

TABLE A-1 Self-described political leanings of under- graduates and faculty members, by type of institution		*Percentage in each political leaning*				
			Doctoral-granting institutions			
	All insti-tutions	*Research and doctoral*		*Doctoral*	
		I	II	I	II
Undergraduates					
Left	5	14	6	6	6
Liberal	39	42	43	36	50
Middle-of-the-road	37	34	30	34	29
Moderately conservative	17	8	20	22	14
Strongly conservative	2	2	1	2	1
TOTAL	100	100	100	100	100
Faculty					
Left	5	7	5	7	3
Liberal	41	49	37	39	43
Middle-of-the-road	27	24	28	26	27
Moderately conservative	24	18	27	25	25
Strongly conservative	3	2	3	3	2
TOTAL	100	100	100	100	100

TABLE A-2 Self-described political leanings of faculty, by age	*Percentage in each political leaning*				
	All ages	*51 or older*	*41–50*	*31–40*	*30 or younger*
Left	5	2	3	6	9
Liberal	41	35	41	43	44
Middle-of-the-road	27	29	28	27	24
Strongly or moderately conservative	27	34	28	24	23
TOTAL	100	100	100	100	100

Comprehensive colleges and universities		Liberal arts colleges		Two-year colleges
I	II	I	II	
4	6	10	5	3
41	36	48	39	36
31	48	26	38	41
21	9	14	16	17
3	1	2	2	3
100	100	100	100	100
4	6	6	4	2
42	35	50	38	30
29	32	23	31	31
22	24	20	25	34
3	3	1	2	3
100	100	100	100	100

TABLE A-3 *Percentage of faculty members who describe themselves as politically "left,"* by field and type of institution*

| | All institutions | Doctoral-granting institutions | | Comprehensive colleges and universities | Liberal arts colleges | Two-year colleges |
		Research and doctoral I	Other doctoral			
Social sciences	10	13	11	8	10	5
Humanities	7	12	9	7	6	4
Physical sciences	4	9	5	3	3	1
Biological sciences	3	5	3	0	1	†
Education/social welfare	3	6	2	2	1	1
Engineering	2	3	2	1	†	†
Health	2	2	1	1	†	†
Law	9	9	†	†	†	†
Other professions	1	3	1	1	0	1
All fields	5	7	5	4	5	2

*Other possible responses: "liberal," "middle-of-the-road," "moderately conservative," "strongly conservative."
†Too few cases.

TABLE A-4 *Percentage of faculty members who describe themselves as politically "left,"* by field and age*

	All ages	51 or older	41–50	31–40	30 or younger
Social sciences	10	4	8	11	16
Humanities	7	2	5	10	14
Physical sciences	4	2	3	5	8
Biological sciences	3	1	2	4	4
Education/social welfare	3	1	3	3	3
Engineering	2	1	2	2	4
Health	2	1	2	2	1
Law	9	†	†	†	†
Other professions	1	0	1	2	2
All fields	5	2	3	6	9

* Other possible responses: "liberal," "middle-of-the-road," "moderately conservative," "strongly conservative."
† Too few cases.

TABLE A-5 *Percentage of faculty members who describe themselves as politically "left,"* * for selected disciplines, by type of institution*

| | All institutions | Doctoral-granting institutions | | Comprehensive colleges and universities | Liberal arts colleges | Two-year colleges |
		Research and doctoral I	Other doctoral			
Sociology	16	25	21	12	11	†
Law	9	9	†	†	†	†
English	9	14	13	8	9	6
Art	6	6	7	4	10	†
Music	2	5	1	3	0	†
Mathematics and statistics	6	13	6	4	5	1
Business and management	1	3	1	0	†	0
Agriculture and forestry	0	0	0	†	†	†

*Other possible responses: "liberal," "middle-of-the-road," "moderately conservative," "strongly conservative."
†Too few cases.

	Percentage who "strongly agree" *or "agree with reservations"**
"Trustees' only responsibility should *be to raise money and gain community* *support"*	
All faculty	45
Type of institution	
Public	
Doctoral-granting institutions	
Research and doctoral I	44
Other doctoral	45
Comprehensive colleges and universities	49
Liberal arts colleges	†
Two-year colleges	41
Private	
Doctoral-granting institutions	
Research and doctoral I	49
Other doctoral	49
Comprehensive colleges and universities	39
Liberal arts colleges	42
Two-year colleges	35
Age of faculty members	
51 or older	35
41 to 50	42
31 to 40	48
30 or younger	62

*Other possible responses: "disagree with reservations," "disagree strongly."
†Too few cases.

TABLE A-7 *Faculty attitudes about collective action and strikes, for faculty in all institutions (in percentages)*

	Strongly agree	Agree with reservations	Disagree with reservations	Strongly disagree	Total
"Collective bargaining by faculty members has no place in a college or university."	18	23	35	24	100
"Faculty unions have a divisive effect on academic life."	20	32	31	17	100
"Faculty members should be more militant in defending their interests."	18	37	31	14	100
"Teaching assistants' unions have a divisive effect on academic life."	20	29	33	18	100
	Definitely yes	Probably yes	Probably not	Definitely not	Total
"Do you feel that there are circumstances in which a strike would be a legitimate means of collective action for faculty members?"	19	27	32	22	100
"Do you feel that there are circumstances in which a strike would be a legitimate means of collective action for teaching assistants?"	17	27	32	24	100

		Doctoral-granting institutions			
TABLE A-8 *Faculty attitudes about collective action and strikes, by type of institution* (in percentages)*	*All insti-tutions*	*Research and doctoral*		*Doctoral*	
		I	II	I	II
"*Collective bargaining by faculty members has no place in a college or university.*"					
"*Strongly disagree*" or "*disagree with reserva-tions*"	59	53	53	56	58
"*Do you feel that there are circumstances in which a strike would be a legitimate means of collective action for faculty members?*"					
"*Definitely yes*" or "*probably yes*"	46	46	43	45	47
"*Faculty unions have a divisive effect on academic life.*"					
"*Strongly disagree*" or "*disagree with reserva-tions*"	48	48	48	50	50
"*Faculty members should be more militant in defending their interests.*"					
"*Strongly agree*" or "*agree with reservations*"	55	56	53	55	58
"*Do you feel that there are circumstances in which a strike would be a legitimate means of collective action for teaching assistants?*"					
"*Definitely yes*" or "*probably yes*"	44	48	43	44	46
"*Teaching assistants' unions have a divisive effect on academic life.*"					
"*Strongly disagree*" or "*disagree with reserva-tions*"	51	49	49	53	54

*Note that all percentages indicate the responses which favor collective action.

Comprehensive colleges and universities		Liberal arts colleges		Two-year colleges
I	II	I	II	
63	66	57	61	68
49	47	45	45	47
49	52	44	52	42
57	57	52	53	53
45	40	42	38	39
53	58	51	50	47

TABLE A-9 *Faculty attitudes about collective bargaining, by age of faculty members and type of institution*

		Doctoral-granting institutions				
Age of faculty members	*All institutions*	*Research and doctoral I*	*Other doctoral*	*Comprehensive colleges and universities*	*Liberal arts colleges*	*Two-year colleges*

Percentage who "strongly disagree" or "disagree with reservations" that collective bargaining by faculty has no place on campus*

Age of faculty members	*All institutions*	*Research and doctoral I*	*Other doctoral*	*Comprehensive colleges and universities*	*Liberal arts colleges*	*Two-year colleges*
51 or older	51	44	47	58	49	64
41–50	57	51	54	60	58	64
31–40	62	57	58	66	65	72
30 or younger	68	64	63	71	69	75
All ages	59	53	55	64	60	68

* Response to the question: "Collective bargaining by faculty members has no place in a college or university." Other possible responses: "strongly agree," "agree with reservations."

TABLE A-10 *Faculty attitudes about collective bargaining, by age of faculty members and tenure status*

Percentage who "strongly disagree" or "disagree with reservations" that collective bargaining by faculty members has no place on campus*

Age of faculty members	*With tenure*	*Without tenure*	*Total*
51 or older	50	55	51
41–50	55	62	57
31–40	60	64	62
30 or younger	62	69	68
All ages	55	64	59

* Response to the question: "Collective bargaining by faculty members has no place in a college or university." Other possible responses: "strongly agree," "agree with reservations."

TABLE A-11
Faculty attitudes about collective bargaining, by age of faculty members and self-described political leanings

Self-described political leaning	Percentage who "strongly disagree" or "disagree with reservations" that collective bargaining by faculty members has no place on campus*				
	All ages	51 or older	41–50	31–40	30 or younger
All political leanings	59	51	57	62	68
Left	88	84	87	88	91
Liberal	68	62	67	70	74
Middle-of-the-road	55	49	52	57	63
Strongly or moderately conservative	45	40	44	48	53

*Response to the question: "Collective bargaining by faculty members has no place in a college or university." Other possible responses: "strongly agree," "agree with reservations."

TABLE A-12
Faculty attitudes about the legitimacy of faculty strikes, by age of faculty members and self-described political leanings

Self-described political leaning	Percentage responding "definitely yes" or "probably yes" that a faculty strike could be legitimate*				
	All ages	51 or older	41–50	31–40	30 or younger
All political leanings	46	32	44	52	59
Left	93	86	90	94	95
Liberal	61	48	60	64	70
Middle-of-the-road	37	28	35	41	48
Strongly or moderately conservative	26	17	24	31	35

*Response to the question: "Do you feel that there are circumstances in which a strike would be a legitimate means of collective action for faculty members." Other possible responses: "probably not," "definitely not."

Type of institution	*Percentage responding "definitely yes" or "probably yes" that a faculty strike could be legitimate**		
	Both public and private	*Public*	*Private*
All types of institutions	46	46	46
Doctoral-granting institutions			
Research and doctoral I	46	45	48
Other doctoral	44	42	48
Comprehensive colleges and universities	48	48	48
Liberal arts colleges	45	†	45
Two-year colleges	47	49	32

* Response to the question: "Do you feel that there are circumstances in which a strike would be a legitimate means of collective action for faculty members?" Other possible responses: "probably not," "definitely not."

† Too few cases.

Ratings of institution	*Percentage who "strongly disagree" or "disagree with reservations" that collective bargaining by faculty has no place on campus**			
	Excellent	*Good*	*Fair*	*Poor*
Effectiveness of campus senate or faculty council	52	55	61	67
Faculty salary levels	51	53	63	71
My own salary	48	55	63	71
The administration	46	55	63	73

*Response to the question: "Collective bargaining by faculty members has no place in a college or university. Other possible responses: "strongly agree," "agree with reservations."

TABLE A-15 *Faculty attitudes about campus governance, by self-described political leanings (in percentages)*

	All political leanings	Left	Liberal	Middle-of-the-road	Strongly or moderately conservative
"There should be faculty representation on the governing board of this institution"					
"Strongly agree"	63	91	72	59	48
"Agree with reservations"	26	9	20	29	34
"Strongly agree" or "agree with reservations"*	89	100	92	88	82
"How would you rate each of the following at your institution?"					
The administration					
"Fair" or "poor"†	47	71	53	42	40
The effectiveness of your campus senate or faculty council					
"Fair" or "poor"†	60	79	63	56	57
"This institution would be better off with fewer administrators"					
"Strongly agree" or "agree with reservations"*	45	64	49	40	42
"Undergraduate education in America would be improved if colleges and universities were governed completely by their faculty and students"					
"Strongly agree" or "agree with reservations"*	40	82	51	32	23

* Other possible responses: "strongly disagree," "disagree with reservations."

Other possible responses: "excellent," "good."

TABLE A-16 *Faculty attitudes* *about campus* *governance, by* *type of institution* *(in percentages)*		Doctoral-granting institutions			
	All *institutions*	*Research* *and doctoral*		*Doctoral*	
		I	II	I	II
"There should be faculty *representation on the* *governing board of this* *institution"*					
"Strongly agree" or "agree *with reservations"**	89	88	88	91	90
"How would you rate each of *the following at your* *institution"* The administration					
"Fair" or "poor"†	47	42	51	54	57
The effectiveness of your *campus senate or faculty* *council*					
"Fair" or "poor"†	60	58	63	69	65
"This institution would be *better off with fewer* *administrators"*					
"Strongly agree" or "agree *with reservations"**	45	43	47	49	57
"Undergraduate education in *America would be improved* *if colleges and universities* *were governed completely by* *their faculty and students"*					
"Strongly agree" or "agree *with reservations"**	40	40	39	40	45

*Other possible responses: "strongly disagree," "disagree with reservations."

† Other possible responses: "excellent," "good."

Comprehensive colleges and universities		Liberal arts colleges		Two-year colleges
I	II	I	II	
91	89	79	87	89
55	42	30	47	45
63	61	41	62	56
48	50	33	32	51
45	35	35	39	36

TABLE A-17
Faculty
evaluations of
their participation
in departmental
affairs and
institutional
government, by
type of institution
(in percentages)

	All insti-tutions	Doctoral-granting institutions			
		Research and doctoral		Doctoral	
		I	II	I	II
"How active are you in your own department's affairs?"					
"Much more than average"	34	30	31	30	37
"Somewhat more than average"	23	22	23	23	24
"About average"	28	26	29	31	25
"Somewhat less than average"	9	13	10	8	7
"Much less than average"	6	9	7	8	7
TOTAL	100	100	100	100	100
"How active are you in the faculty government of your institution, (committee membership, etc.)?"					
"Much more than average"	15	11	11	12	15
"Somewhat more than average"	16	12	15	13	16
"About average"	26	23	23	25	25
"Somewhat less than average"	23	27	28	24	23
"Much less than average"	20	27	23	26	21
TOTAL	100	100	100	100	100
"How much opportunity do you feel you have to influence the policies of your department?"					
"A great deal"	33	27	29	29	32
"Quite a bit"	28	27	30	26	27
"Some"	32	35	33	37	31
"None"	7	11	8	8	10
TOTAL	100	100	100	100	100
"How much opportunity do you feel you have to influence the policies of your institution?"					
"A great deal"	5	3	3	3	3
"Quite a bit"	13	9	10	9	11
"Some"	48	47	47	45	45
"None"	34	41	40	43	41
TOTAL	100	100	100	100	100

Comprehensive colleges and universities		Liberal arts colleges		Two-year colleges
I	II	I	II	
35	38	36	39	39
23	24	26	22	22
27	28	28	27	30
10	7	7	7	6
5	3	3	5	3
100	100	100	100	100
15	21	19	21	20
12	19	15	20	22
30	28	24	30	26
25	20	24	15	19
18	12	18	14	13
100	100	100	100	100
30	35	49	46	36
27	30	23	24	32
34	32	24	26	26
9	3	4	4	6
100	100	100	100	100
4	8	10	12	7
11	13	23	17	19
48	48	47	50	54
37	31	20	21	20
100	100	100	100	100

TABLE A-18 Faculty attitudes about campus governance, by whether collective bargaining has a place in higher education (in percentages)		Faculty who "strongly agree" or "agree with reservations" that "collective bargaining by faculty members has no place in a college or university"	Faculty who "strongly disagree" or "disagree with reservations" that "collective bargaining by faculty members has no place in a college or university"
"There should be faculty representation on the governing board of this institution"			
"Strongly agree" or "agree with reservations"*		82	93
"Undergraduate education in America would be improved if colleges and universities were governed completely by their faculty and students"			
"Strongly agree" or "agree with reservations"*		29	47

* Other possible responses: "strongly disagree" or "disagree with reservations."

TABLE A-19 Type of faculty appointments,* by type of institution (in percentages)			Doctoral-granting institutions			
		All institutions	Research and doctoral		Doctoral	
			I	II	I	II
"Regular with tenure"		49	52	52	50	46
"Regular without tenure"		47	43	44	45	51
"Acting"		2	2	2	2	1
"Visiting"		2	3	3	3	2
	TOTAL	100	100	100	100	100

*Response to the question, "What kind of appointment do you have here?"

Comprehensive colleges and universities		Liberal arts colleges		Two-year colleges
I	II	I	II	
46	54	49	42	54
50	42	45	53	43
2	2	2	2	2
2	2	4	3	1
100	100	100	100	100

TABLE A-20
Attitudes toward student participation: comparison of faculty, graduate students, and undergraduates, for all institutions (in percentages)

| | | *Percentage who say* undergraduates *should have* "control" or "voting power on committees" * | |
Area of decision making	*Faculty*	*Graduate students*	*Under-graduates*
Residence hall regulations			78
Student discipline	64	53	72
Provision and content of courses	14	25	43
Degree requirements	13	16	27
Admissions policy	14	13	25
Faculty appointment and promotion	6	11	23

Percentage who say graduate students should have "control" or "voting power on committees"*		Percentage who say undergraduates should have "control" or "voting power on committees" or "formal consultation†			Percentage who say graduate students should have "control" or "voting power on committees" or "formal consultation"†	
Faculty	Graduate students	Faculty	Graduate students	Under-graduates	Faculty	Graduate students
				93		
60	53	88	77	91	81	77
24	42	49	62	77	65	79
21	29	43	46	62	55	63
16	22	38	38	53	42	52
11	21	21	30	48	30	47

* Other possible responses: "formal consultation," "informal consultation," "little or no role."

† Other possible responses: "informal consultation," "little or no role."

NOTE: Questions about the role of graduate students asked about "graduate courses."

Questions about the role of undergraduates asked about "Bachelor's degree requirements," while questions on graduate students asked about "advanced degree requirements."

Questions about the role of undergraduates asked about "undergraduate admissions policy," while questions on graduate students asked about "departmental graduate admissions policy."

		Percentage responding "control" or		
TABLE A-21 *Faculty and undergraduate attitudes about undergraduate participation, by field: percentages favoring at least voting power on committees*		*All fields*	*Social sciences*	*Humanities*	*Physical sciences*
	"What role do you believe undergraduates should play in decisions on the following?"				
	"Student discipline"				
	Faculty	64	73	68	64
	Undergraduates	72	79	74	71
	"Provision and content of courses"				
	Faculty	14	21	17	11
	Undergraduates	43	54	50	39
	"Bachelor's degree requirements"				
	Faculty	13	22	18	9
	Undergraduates	27	37	34	23
	"Undergraduate admissions policy"				
	Faculty	14	25	17	12
	Undergraduates	25	27	30	25
	"Faculty appointment and promotion"				
	Faculty	6	11	9	3
	Undergraduates	23	33	24	21

"voting power on committees"						
Biological sciences	Education/ social welfare	Engineering	Health	Law	Other professions	All professions
66	62	55	57	79	59	
77	75					71
7	16	3	16	27	9	
43	45					36
12	14	2	14	14	7	
25	28					22
12	16	3	10	16	8	
27	23					21
2	6	1	4	6	4	
19	24					15

TABLE A-22
Faculty and
undergraduate
attitudes about
undergraduate
participation,
by field:
percentages
favoring at least
formal
consultation

	Percentage responding "control,"			
	All fields	*Social sciences*	*Humanities*	*Physical sciences*
"What role do you believe undergraduates should play in decisions on the following?"				
"Student discipline"				
Faculty	88	92	90	88
Undergraduates	91	96	93	91
"Provision and content of courses"				
Faculty	49	57	53	43
Undergraduates	77	85	79	75
"Bachelor's degree requirements"				
Faculty	43	54	48	37
Undergraduates	62	73	64	60
"Undergraduate admissions policy"				
Faculty	38	50	43	32
Undergraduates	53	58	54	55
"Faculty appointment and promotion"				
Faculty	21	30	27	17
Undergraduates	48	59	53	48

"voting power on committees," or "formal consultation"

Biological sciences	Education/ social welfare	Engineering	Health	Law	Other professions	All professions
91	86	80	87	95	83	
94	91					90
46	52	33	57	73	44	
75	81					72
46	42	24	39	52	36	
52	66					57
38	38	23	34	47	29	
47	56					49
16	20	13	20	27	12	
54	44					40

TABLE A-23 *Faculty and* *graduate student* *attitudes about* *graduate student* *participation,* *by field:* *percentages* *favoring at least* *voting power on* *committees*		*Percentage responding "control"*		
	All *fields*	*Social* *sciences*	*Humanities*	*Physical* *sciences*
"What role do you believe *graduate students should* *play in decisions on the* *following?"*				
"Student discipline"				
Faculty	60	67	65	57
Graduate students	53	65	58	54
"Provision and content *of graduate courses"*				
Faculty	24	32	28	17
Graduate students	42	57	53	36
"Advanced degree *requirements"*				
Faculty	21	30	26	13
Graduate students	29	46	39	20
"Departmental graduate *admissions policy"*				
Faculty	16	24	21	9
Graduate students	22	37	32	13
"Faculty appointment *and promotion"*				
Faculty	11	16	17	7
Graduate students	21	35	29	15

or "voting power on committees"

Biological sciences	Education/ social welfare	Engineering	Health	Law	Other professions
58	57	51	59	79	56
47	48	43	64	72	46
14	27	11	30	33	17
41	41	30	44	60	31
16	20	6	22	24	16
29	30	14	24	33	21
11	17	5	15	17	9
18	23	12	22	27	12
6	10	4	9	9	6
16	18	14	20	27	15

TABLE A-24 *Faculty and* *graduate student* *attitudes about* *graduate student* *participation,* *by field:* *percentages* *favoring at least* *formal* *consultation*		*Percentage responding "control," "voting power*		
		All *fields*	*Social* *sciences*	*Humanities*	*Physical* *sciences*

	All fields	Social sciences	Humanities	Physical sciences
"What role do you believe graduate students should play in decisions on the following?"				
"Student discipline"				
Faculty	81	85	86	79
Graduate students	77	84	74	77
"Provision and content of graduate courses"				
Faculty	65	71	69	58
Graduate students	79	84	81	77
"Advanced degree requirements"				
Faculty	54	63	62	42
Graduate students	63	75	70	56
"Departmental graduate admissions policy"				
Faculty	42	53	50	32
Graduate students	52	63	64	47
"Faculty appointment and promotion"				
Faculty	30	39	39	24
Graduate students	47	62	58	42

1 committees," or "formal consultation"

ological iences	Education/ social welfare	Engineering	Health	Law	Other professions
82	79	75	83	91	76
78	73	72	86	90	74
61	67	47	73	74	61
86	74	83	87	91	75
52	58	31	54	54	52
74	63	45	68	73	57
40	43	24	44	45	36
49	52	44	57	59	42
24	28	19	30	31	21
43	44	39	51	59	37

TABLE A-25
Faculty, graduate, and undergraduate attitudes toward student participation, by type of institution

	All insti-tutions	Doctoral-granting institution.			
		Research and doctoral		Doctoral	
		I	II	I	
"In decisions on student discipline, *what role do you believe* undergraduates *should play?"*					
Percentage responding "control" or "voting power"					
Faculty	64	64	66	62	6
Graduates	53	62	54	55	5
Undergraduates	72	80	77	81	8
"In decisions on student discipline, *what role do you believe* graduate *students should play?"*					
Percentage responding "control" or "voting power"					
Faculty	60	63	61	55	6
Graduates	53	63	54	54	5
"In decisions on the provision and content *of courses, what role do you believe* undergraduates *should play?"*					
Percentage responding "control" or "voting power"					
Faculty	14	14	14	13	1
Graduates	25	31	24	24	2
Undergraduates	43	54	42	44	5
"In decisions on the provision and content of graduate courses, *what role do you believe* graduate students should play?"*					
Percentage responding "control" or "voting power"					
Faculty	24	23	22	18	2
Graduates	42	51	44	43	4

Comprehensive colleges and universities		Liberal arts colleges		Two-year colleges
I	II	I	II	
67	67	74	69	54
47	47			
75	80	90	81	60
61	62	67	64	50
45	51	*	*	*
15	10	18	16	12
23	20			
44	58	51	48	34
25	18	28	26	25
39	34	*	*	*

TABLE A-25
(Continued)

	All institutions	Doctoral-granting institutions			
		Research and doctoral		Doctoral	
		I	II	I	II
"In decisions on bachelor's degree requirements, *what role do you believe* undergraduates *should* play?"*					
Percentage responding "control" or "voting power"					
Faculty	13	13	16	11	13
Graduates	16	20	16	15	11
Undergraduates	27	37	33	28	28
"In decisions on advanced degree requirements, *what role do you believe* graduate *students should* play?"*					
Percentage responding "control" or "voting power"					
Faculty	21	19	19	15	18
Graduates	29	36	29	30	29
"In decisions on undergraduate admissions policy, *what role do you believe* undergraduates *should* play?"*					
Percentage responding "control" or "voting power"					
Faculty	14	12	14	12	11
Graduates	13	17	13	13	12
Undergraduates	25	26	20	26	23
"In decisions on departmental graduate admissions policy, *what role do you believe* graduate *students should* play?"*					
Percentage responding "control" or "voting power"					
Faculty	16	14	15	11	14
Graduates	22	26	22	23	18

Comprehensive colleges and universities		Liberal arts colleges		Two-year colleges
I	II	I	II	
14	8	20	16	9
14	11			
30	36	42	33	18
21	15	24	24	23
26	23	*	*	*
17	12	19	19	12
11	11			
24	31	29	28	25
18	14	20	20	15
22	20	*	*	*

	All insti- tutions	Doctoral-granting institutions			
TABLE A-25 (Continued)		Research and doctoral		Doctoral	
		I	II	I	II
"In decisions on faculty appointment and promotion, *what role do you believe* undergraduates *should play?"*					
Percentage responding "control" or "voting power"					
Faculty	6	5	6	5	6
Graduates	11	13	9	13	13
Undergraduates	23	36	20	23	32
"In decisions on faculty appointment and promotion, *what role do you believe* graduate *students should play?"*					
Percentage responding "control" or "voting power"					
Faculty	11	9	9	8	10
Graduates	21	25	21	22	21

*Too few cases or does not apply.

Comprehensive colleges and universities		Liberal arts colleges		Two-year colleges
I	II	I	II	
7	7	7	6	4
9	9			
22	28	29	25	19
12	10	13	15	14
19	16	*	*	*

TABLE A-26 *Faculty attitudes about the decision-making role of undergraduates, by age of faculty members*

	Percentage responding "formal consultation," "voting power on committees," or "control"				
	All ages	*51 or older*	*41–50*	*31–40*	*30 or younger*
"What role do you believe undergraduates *should play* in decisions on the following?"					
"Student discipline"	88	81	88	90	92
"Provision and content of courses"	49	38	48	53	62
"Bachelor's degree requirements"	43	32	39	47	57
"Undergraduate admissions policy"	38	26	38	41	47
"Faculty appointment and promotion"	21	13	19	23	32
	Percentage responding "voting power on committees" or "control"				
	All ages	*51 or older*	*41–50*	*31–40*	*30 or younger*
"Student discipline"	64	53	65	69	72
"Provision and content of courses"	14	9	13	16	21
"Bachelor's degree requirements"	13	8	11	15	21
"Undergraduate admissions policy"	14	8	14	16	19
"Faculty appointment and promotion"	6	4	5	6	11

TABLE A-27 *Faculty attitudes about the decision-making role of graduate students, by age of faculty members*

	Percentage responding "formal consultation," "voting power," or "control"				
	All ages	*51 or older*	*41–50*	*31–40*	*30 or younger*
"What role do you believe graduate students should play in decisions on the following?"					
"Student discipline"	81	73	82	85	85
"Provision and content of graduate courses"	65	52	63	69	78
"Advanced degree requirements"	55	44	52	59	65
"Departmental graduate admissions policy"	42	32	41	46	52
"Faculty appointment and promotion"	30	20	27	33	42
	Percentage responding "voting power" or "control"				
	All ages	*51 or older*	*41–50*	*31–40*	*30 or younger*
"Student discipline"	60	47	61	65	68
"Provision and content of graduate courses"	24	16	20	26	35
"Advanced degree requirements"	21	12	18	23	32
"Departmental graduate admissions policy"	16	9	14	18	24
"Faculty appointment and promotion"	11	7	9	12	18

TABLE A-28
Faculty attitudes
about graduate
student
participation, by
whether their
departments
have increased
graduate student
participation

	Percentage responding that graduate students should have "control," "voting power" or "formal consultation"	
	Faculty who say that their departments have increased graduate student participation*	Faculty who say that their departments have not increased graduate student participation†
"What role do you believe graduate students should play in decisions on the following?"		
"Student discipline"	85	79
"Provision and content of graduate courses"	70	56
"Advanced degree requirements"	58	45
"Departmental graduate admissions policy"	45	32
"Faculty appointment and promotion"	30	23

* Respondents who "strongly agree" or "agree with reservations" to the question: "My department has taken steps to increase graduate student participation in its decisions."

† Respondents who "strongly disagree" or "disagree with reservations" to the question: "My department has taken steps to increase graduate student participation in its decisions."

TABLE A-29
Faculty attitudes
about the use of
student
evaluations in
faculty
promotions, by
type of institution

	All institutions	Doctoral-granting institutions			
		Research and doctoral		Doctoral	
		I	II	I	II
"Faculty promotions should be based in part on formal student evaluations of their teachers."					
Percentage responding "strongly agree"	14	13	13	14	13
Percentage responding "agree with reservations"	41	40	43	43	45
Percentage responding "disagree with reservations"	30	30	30	27	29
Percentage responding "strongly disagree"	15	17	14	16	13
TOTAL	100	100	100	100	100

Comprehensive colleges and universities		Liberal arts colleges		Two-year colleges
I	II	I	II	
15	16	17	15	14
39	35	44	46	41
29	33	28	27	32
17	16	11	12	13
100	100	100	100	100

TABLE A-30 *Undergraduate attitudes about the decision-making role of undergraduates, by self-described political leanings*

	Percentage responding "formal consultation," "voting power on committees," or "control"				
	All political leanings	*Left*	*Liberal*	*Middle-of-the-road*	*Strongly or moderately conservative*
"What role do you believe under-graduates should play in decisions on the following?"					
"Student discipline"	91	95	93	91	85
"Provision and content of courses"	77	90	82	76	63
"Bachelor's degree requirements"	62	89	67	61	44
"Undergraduate admissions policy"	53	83	58	51	40
"Faculty appointment and promotion"	48	90	55	42	36
	Percentage responding "voting power on committees" or "control"				
	All political leanings	*Left*	*Liberal*	*Middle-of-the-road*	*Strongly or moderately conservative*
"Student discipline"	72	88	81	69	58
"Provision and content of courses"	43	66	51	40	26
"Bachelor's degree requirements"	27	55	33	23	16
"Undergraduate admissions policy"	25	53	31	20	19
"Faculty appointment and promotion"	23	70	28	15	13

TABLE A-31   *Faculty attitudes about undergraduate participation, by self-described political leanings of faculty members*

	Percentage responding "formal consultation," "voting power on committees," or "control"				
	All political leanings	Left	Liberal	Middle-of-the-road	Strongly or moderately conservative
"What role do you believe under-graduates should play in decisions on the following?"					
"Student discipline"	88	96	94	86	79
"Provision and content of courses"	49	82	60	43	34
"Bachelor's degree requirements"	43	81	53	40	23
"Undergraduate admissions policy"	38	76	49	32	20
"Faculty appointment and promotion"	21	62	28	15	9

	Percentage responding "voting power on committees" or "control"				
	All political leanings	Left	Liberal	Middle-of-the-road	Strongly or moderately conservative
"Student discipline"	64	91	76	59	48
"Provision and content of courses"	14	45	20	9	5
"Bachelor's degree requirements"	13	48	18	9	4
"Undergraduate admissions policy"	14	47	19	10	5
"Faculty appointment and promotion"	6	33	7	4	2

TABLE A-32 *Faculty attitudes about the decision-making role of graduate students, by self-described political leanings of faculty members*

	Percentage responding "formal consultation," "voting power on committees," or "control"				
	All political leanings	Left	Liberal	Middle-of-the-road	Strongly or moderately conservative
"What role do you believe graduate students should play in decisions on the following?"					
"Student discipline"	81	95	88	79	72
"Provision and content of graduate courses"	65	89	73	61	52
"Advanced degree requirements"	55	85	63	51	40
"Departmental graduate admissions policy"	42	78	52	37	26
"Faculty appointment and promotion"	30	67	37	26	16
	Percentage responding "voting power on committees" or "control"				
	All political leanings	Left	Liberal	Middle-of-the-road	Strongly or moderately conservative
"Student discipline"	60	91	71	55	44
"Provision and content of graduate courses"	24	60	30	18	12
"Advanced degree requirements"	21	55	27	16	9
"Departmental graduate admissions policy"	16	49	21	11	6
"Faculty appointment and promotion"	11	39	14	7	4

Appendix B: Carnegie Commission Classification of Institutions of Higher Education, 1970

This classification includes all institutions listed in the U.S. Office of Education's *Advance Report on Opening Fall Enrollment in Higher Education: Institutional Data, 1970*. Whenever a campus of a multicampus institution is listed separately, it is included as a separate institution in our classification. In a few instances, the Office of Education includes all campuses of an institution in a single listing, and in such cases the institution is treated as a single entry in our classification. Our classification includes 2,827 institutions, as compared with the Office of Education total of 2,565 for 1970. The difference is explained by the fact that, for purposes of obtaining the total number of institutions, we have treated each campus as an institution, whereas the Office of Education treats multicampus systems as single institutions *for purposes of obtaining the total number of institutions.*

Another significant problem arises in connection with medical schools, schools of engineering, schools of business administration, and law schools. These institutions appear separately only if they are listed as separate institutions in *Opening Fall Enrollment.* Most of these professional schools are not listed separately, since their enrollment is included in the enrollment of the parent university or university campus. This is true even in a number of instances in which the professional school is not located on the main campus of the university, but on a separate campus, e.g., Johns Hopkins University School of Medicine.

The classification includes five main groups of institutions and a number of subcategories, or 18 categories in all. They are as follows:

1. Doctoral-granting institutions

1.1 Research and doctoral-granting universities I These are the 50 leading institutions in terms of federal financial support of academic science in at least two of the three years, 1965–66, 1966–67, and 1967–68, provided they awarded at least 50 Ph.D.'s (plus M.D.'s if a medical school was on the same campus) in 1967–68. Rockefeller University was included because of the high quality of its research and doctoral training, even though it did not meet these criteria.

1.2 Research and doctoral-granting universities II These institutions were on the list of 100 leading institutions in terms of federal financial support in at least two out of three of the above three years and awarded at least 50 Ph.D.'s (plus M.D.'s if a medical school was on the same campus) in 1967–68, or they were among the leading 50 institutions in terms of number of Ph.D.'s (plus M.D.'s if a medical school was on the same campus) awarded in that year. In addition, a few institutions that did not quite meet these criteria, but which had graduate programs of high quality and with impressive promise for future development, were included in 1.2.

1.3 Doctoral-granting universities I These institutions awarded 40 or more Ph.D.'s in 1967–68 (plus M.D.'s if a medical school was on the same campus) or received at least $4 million in total federal financial support in 1967–68. No institution is included that granted less than 20 Ph.D.'s (plus M.D.'s if a medical school was on the same campus), regardless of the amount of federal financial support it received.

1.4 Doctoral-granting universities II These institutions awarded at least 10 Ph.D.'s in 1967–68, with the exception of a few new doctoral-granting institutions which may be expected to increase the number of Ph.D.'s awarded within a few years.

2. Comprehensive colleges and universities

2.1 Comprehensive colleges and universities I This group includes institutions that offered a liberal arts program as well as several other programs, such as engineering, business administration, etc. Many of them offered master's degrees, but all lacked a doctoral program or had only an extremely limited doctoral program. All institutions in this group had at least two professional or occupational programs and enrolled at least 2,000 students in 1970. If an institution's enrollment was smaller than this, it was not considered very comprehensive.

2.2   Comprehensive colleges and universities II   This list includes state colleges and some private colleges that offered a liberal arts program and at least one professional or occupational program, such as teacher training or nursing. Many of the institutions in this group are former teachers colleges that have recently broadened their programs to include a liberal arts curriculum. Private institutions with less than 1,500 students and public institutions with less than 1,000 students in 1970 are not included, even though they may offer a selection of programs, because, with small enrollments, they cannot be regarded as comprehensive. Such institutions are classified as liberal arts colleges. The differentiation between private and public institutions is based on the fact that public state colleges are experiencing relatively rapid increases in enrollment and are likely to have at least 1,500 students within a few years even if they did not in 1970. Most of the state colleges with relatively few students were established quite recently.

3.   Liberal arts colleges

3.1   Liberal arts colleges I   These colleges scored 58 or above on Astin's selectivity index (Alexander W. Astin, *Who Goes Where to College?*, Science Research Associates, Chicago, 1965), *or* they were included among the 200 leading baccalaureate-granting institutions in terms of numbers of their graduates receiving Ph.D.'s at 40 leading doctoral-granting institutions, 1920–1966 (National Academy of Sciences, *Doctorate Recipients from United States Universities, 1958–1966*).

   The distinction between a liberal arts college and a comprehensive college is not sharp or clear-cut. Some of the institutions in this group have modest occupational programs but a strong liberal arts tradition. A good example is Oberlin, which awarded 91 Mus.B. degrees out of a total of 564 bachelor's degrees in 1967, as well as 31 M.A.T. degrees out of a total of 41 master's degrees. Its enrollment in 1970 was 2,670. Or, consider two Pennsylvania institutions, Lafayette and Swarthmore. The former awarded 113 B.S. degrees in engineering in 1967 out of a total of 349 bachelor's degrees and has been classified in our comprehensive colleges II group. Its enrollment in 1970 was 2,161. Swarthmore has an engineering program leading to a B.S. degree, but it awarded only 11 B.S. degrees out of a total of 250 bachelor's degrees in 1967 and had a 1970 enrollment of 1,164. Swarthmore has a strong liberal arts tradition and did not meet our minimum enrollment criterion for a private college to be classified as a comprehensive college II in 1970, so its case was clear, but our decisions in the cases of Oberlin and Lafayette had to be at least partly judgmental.

3.2 Liberal arts colleges—selectivity II These institutions include all the liberal arts colleges that did not meet our criteria for inclusion in the first group of liberal arts colleges. Again, in many cases, the distinction between some of the larger colleges in this group and in the comprehensive colleges groups is not sharp and clear-cut, but is necessarily partly a matter of judgment.

In addition, as we pointed out, many liberal arts colleges are extensively involved in teacher training, but future teachers tend to receive their degrees in arts and sciences fields, rather than in education.

4. All two-year colleges and institutes

5. Professional schools and other specialized institutions

5.1 Theological seminaries, bible colleges, and other institutions offering degrees in religion (not including colleges with religious affiliations offering a liberal arts program as well as degrees in religion).

5.2 Medical schools and medical centers As indicated above, this list includes only those that are listed as separate campuses in *Opening Fall Enrollment*. In some instances, the medical center includes other health professional schools, e.g., dentistry, pharmacy, nursing.

5.3   Other separate health professional schools

5.4   Schools of engineering and technology   Technical institutes are included only if they award a bachelor's degree and if their program is limited exclusively or almost exclusively to technical fields of study.

5.5   Schools of business and management   Business schools are included only if they award a bachelor's or higher degree and if their program is limited exclusively or almost exclusively to a business curriculum.

5.6   Schools of art, music, design, etc.

5.7   Schools of law

5.8   Teachers colleges   Teachers colleges are included only if they do not have a liberal arts program.

5.9   Other specialized institutions   Includes graduate centers, maritime academies, military institutes (lacking a liberal arts program), and miscellaneous.

Appendix G: Summary of Recommendations in Reports of Institutional Committees and Other Commissions or Associations

The proposals of governance committees in several institutions and the recommendations or statements of a variety of commissions and associations are presented in this appendix in order to amplify textual material and to suggest different approaches to the complex problems discussed. The recommendations included have not all been adopted. The inclusion of statements by other groups does not necessarily imply our concurrence with the ideas expressed. Rather, our intention is to provide the reader with a range of relevant information. Although the full statements or reports of the various groups often cover many subjects, the material presented here is excerpted and restricted to topics covered in the text of this report.

With the exception of the section on campuswide councils, all statements are quotations. For campuswide councils, summaries of the structures and powers of existing or recommended councils have been prepared by the Carnegie Commission staff. Descriptions of existing councils have been updated to reflect current practices.

The recommendations summarized here cover the following topics:

1. Boards of trustees

2. Presidents

3. Faculty participation

4. Collective bargaining

5. Faculty appointment

6. Faculty promotion and tenure

7. Student participation
8. Student evaluation of faculty
9. Campuswide councils and senates
10. Openness of decision making and communications

Recommendations are cited from the following sources:

- Harvard University, the University Committee on Governance. Several reports cited individually. (Hereafter referred to as Harvard.)

- Princeton University, *The Governing of Princeton University*, final report of the Special Committee on the Structure of the University, 1970. (Hereafter referred to as Princeton.)

- Stanford University, *Government of the University*, the Study of Education at Stanford, 1969. (Hereafter referred to as Stanford.)

- University of Toronto, *Toward Community in University Government*, report of the Commission on the Government of the University of Toronto, 1970. (Hereafter referred to as Toronto.)

- University of Utah, *Report of the University of Utah Commission to Study Tenure*, 1971. (Hereafter referred to as Utah.)

- Yale University, Study Commission on Governance, *Final Report*, 1971. (Hereafter referred to as Yale.)

- American Association of Higher Education–National Education Association Task Force on Faculty Representation and Academic Negotiations, *Faculty Participation in Academic Governance*, 1967. (Hereafter referred to as AAHE-NEA Task Force.)

- American Association of State Colleges and Universities, *Academic Freedom and Responsibility, and Academic Tenure*, 1971. (Hereafter referred to as American Association of State Colleges and Universities.)

- American Council on Education, *Report of the Special Committee on Campus Tensions*, 1970. (Hereafter referred to as ACE.)

- The American Academy of Arts and Sciences, Assembly on University Goals and Governance, *A First Report*, 1971. (Hereafter referred to as American Academy of Arts and Sciences, Assembly on University Goals and Governance.)

- Association of American Colleges, *Statement on Financial Exigency and Staff Reduction*, 1971. (Hereafter referred to as Association of American Colleges.)

- Great Britain, *Joint Statement from the Committee of Vice Chancellors and Principals and the National Union of Students*. (From *Minerva*, "Reports and Documents" Vol. VII, Nos. 1-2, Autumn–Winter 1968–69, pp. 67–69.) (Hereafter referred to as British Joint Statement.)

- *The Report of the President's Commission on Campus Unrest,* 1970. (Hereafter referred to as Scranton Commission.)

- White House Conference on Youth, *Task Force Recommendations, Education,* 1971. (Hereafter referred to as White House Conference on Youth.)

Additional information about campuswide councils and senates was obtained from:

- Columbia University, *A Plan for Participation: Proposal for a University Senate with Faculty, Student, Administration and other Membership,* 1969.

- Ohio State University, *A Proposal for the Establishment of a University Senate for The Ohio State University,* as amended through April 1972.

- Princeton University, *A Proposal to Establish The Council of the Princeton University Community,* 1969.

- University of Minnesota, *Constitution and By-Laws of the University Senate,* 1969.

- University of New Hampshire, *Report of the Committee on Government Organization,* 1969.

- *The University of Toronto Act,* 1971.

- Harvard University, The University Committee on Governance, *Tentative Recommendations Concerning a University Senate and The Council of Deans,* 1972.

1. BOARDS OF TRUSTEES

Stanford:

The primary responsibility of the Board of Trustees should be to ensure the long-run welfare of the University and to support the University in its relationships with other social institutions and with its external constituencies. To free itself for more effective performance of this essential role, the Board should, in concert with other members of the University, reexamine its own policies and procedures in order to make substantial explicit delegations of operating responsibility.

All meetings of the Board should take place on the campus.

Meetings of the Board should be reduced in frequency and increased in duration so as to afford trustees a deeper familiarity with the University.

The Board of Trustees should seek to increase the diversity of its membership with respect to such factors as age, occupation, cultural and racial background, and place of residence. This effort should give a high priority to adding members who are actively engaged in teaching and scholarship at other universities and colleges.

The Nominating Committee of the Board should be enlarged to include members of the Stanford faculty, student body, and alumni.

Trustees should be elected to five-year terms renewable not more than twice.

Membership on Board committees should include Stanford faculty members and students as well as trustees.

One or more Stanford faculty members with relevant expertise should serve as members of the Board's Committee on Investments.

The President and possibly the Provost should be *ex officio* members of the Board.

The Board, in concert with other members of the University should study and consider: enlarging the Board to perhaps double its present size; direct election of one or more trustees by each of the following groups—the faculty, the student body, the alumni; creating an Executive Committee to maintain continuity between meetings.

Toronto:
[Editorial note: The Toronto Commission recommended the establishment of a single governing council with the duties and powers of both the board and the senate. Such a body has been in operation since July 1972.]

That there be established a sole governing authority with final control over all financial and academic matters within the University of Toronto to be named the Governing Council. That the membership of the Governing Council of sixty-six members be distributed in the following manner:

- 20 lay members
- 20 elected students [5 graduate students, 15 undergraduate students]
- 20 elected academic staff
- 6 *ex officio* members

The Commission recommends that graduates of the university elect ten members to the Governing Council.

American Academy of Arts and Sciences, Assembly on University Goals and Governance:
The ultimate legal authority in most contemporary American colleges and universities resides in a lay governing board. The idea that higher education is too important to be left to educators and students alone, and that it requires surveillance by the larger society, is implied by this arrangement. Because of the importance of trustees, they ought to be chosen on the basis of their capacity for deliberation, judgment, and vision. These attributes do not run counter to fund-raising ability and devotion to the institution.

The principal functions of the governing board ought to include: to join with the president in planning the long-range future of the institution (the faculty can rarely transcend itself in this matter, and students generally have too short a time-perspective); to select a president with the cooperation of those that have reason to be interested in the appointment; to preserve and improve the financial position of the institution; to link the institution with public and other outside agencies in such a way that will advance the interests of faculty and students.

Though governing boards should not be selected on a Noah's Ark principle, certain groups (blacks, for example) are rarely included; women are least represented, considering the proportion of women students. Both ought to be significantly represented; if represented, they would enhance the general influence of the board, bring new perspectives, and, in some instances, might possibly improve their fund-raising capacity. At most institutions, board members ought to have renewable term rather than life appointments.

Faculty and students serving on the governing boards of their own institutions might lead boards into day-to-day academic decisions that ought in fact to be delegated. However, governing boards should often include professors and administrators from other institutions. Recent alumni are often closer to the perceptions of students than others, and should be considered for board positions. Faculty and students ought to have the opportunity to nominate outside trustees, though not necessarily to select them. The opportunity to nominate by a petition signed by a designated number of faculty or students—alumni frequently have such a privilege—ought to be experimented with. Faculty senates, student governments, employee organizations ought all to have means available for communicating with the governing board.

Boards of trustees have often been effective buffers against political and other pressures directed at colleges and universities. Today, however, boards are sometimes the conduits of these pressures, serving only to exacerbate already difficult situations. The buffer role ought to be reinforced, particularly in those state institutions where political pressures are especially strong.

Princeton:

That committees of the Board of Trustees and committees of the Council of the Princeton University Community hold joint meetings for an exchange of views on general or controversial issues.

That the Board of Trustees and its committees make some of their sessions public, in whole or in part.

That the Board of Trustees regularly make public statements of the reasons for its actions on major issues.

ACE:
Every institution should have carefully framed bylaws, subject to periodic re-examination, that set forth the board's essential authority and responsibility and defines its procedures. Periodic review of the bylaws will benefit from outside counsel and from attention to what other institutions are doing. Even such basic matters as the board's mode of selection and appointment, size, composition, term of office, should be re-examined. For example, switching to popular election of boards might dissuade men of detached viewpoint from applying, but self-perpetuating boards of lifetime members have faults as well. Institutions with the latter system should consider that fixed terms for trustees would preserve detachment and continuity, while at the same time ensuring periodic rejuvenation of the board.

Students, faculty, and others need to be well informed about how decisions are made in their institution and the reasons for policies that are decided. The bylaws of the trustees should be accessible to all members of the academic community and to concerned outsiders, as should agenda of each meeting. When major decisions are made, boards should promptly issue reports which explain reasons for the actions taken. Boards must have well-publicized rules governing the submission of petitions, and adequate procedures for prompt consideration of them.

Boards should make more effective use of special committees and other mechanisms through which they and representatives of students, faculty, staff, and alumni can communicate more readily.

In the matter of finances, ways must be found to re-examine institutional priorities so that there will be both wider opportunity for involvement and a greater sharing of responsibility among students, faculty, staff, and others.

Delegation of responsibility and accountability does not absolve trustees of the need to be well informed about the institution's programs and to be serious students of higher education generally. Presidents and others who influence heavily the content of the board agenda should focus it more on educational issues and less on fiscal and housekeeping chores.

Although anything resembling a quota scheme of representation in board membership should be avoided, there should be a greater diversity of age, occupation, and other salient individual characteristics that might broaden horizons and present other points of view. Some boards of trustees may wish to consider adding student and faculty members from their own institutions; other boards, desiring to avoid the possible conflicts of interests that may arise from such participation, can achieve broadened viewpoints by adding members drawn from other institutions. Ultimately, the evolving nature of higher education may require re-examination and reassessment of the authority and functions of trustees in the governance of the university, along with reappraisal of a need to delegate some of their authority to other groups on the campus.

Scranton Commission:

Trustees have a particular responsibility to interpret and explain their institution to the larger society. They should attempt to inform the public about the institution's values, goals, complexities, and changes. They should defend academic freedom and the right of students, teachers, and guest speakers to espouse unpopular views. They should attempt to help the public understand the underlying causes of student unrest and to prevent punitive or counterproductive public policies toward higher education.

Trustees have an equally important responsibility to assure that their university maintains its central commitments to teaching, to research, and to the preservation of academic freedom against internal erosion. Specifically, this means discouraging excessive service commitments by the university, resisting internal politicization of the university, supporting academic reform, and encouraging improvement in university governance.

To be effective in these difficult roles, trustees must be familiar with the institution they oversee and with the concerns of its constituents. They should read campus publications and be in contact with students, faculty members, and administrators. Those unable to find time for these activities will be unable to perform their role well.

Yale:

At such a time as seems appropriate to ask for legislative revision of the charter given to Yale University by the state of Connecticut, the Commission believes, the Corporation should seek the following changes in the charter:

- Student-faculty election of two trustees—By adding to the trustees or replacing existing seats, two trustees should be elected to the Corporation by an electorate composed of Yale faculty and students, each trustee to serve a six-year term, with the term of one to begin three years after the term of the other. A nominating committee should place at least two names of candidates before the electorate. . . . For calculating the percentage of votes received by each candidate an average should be taken of the percentage of student votes and percentage of faculty votes for each candidate.[1]

- Twelve-year terms for Successor Trustees—Successor Trustees should be limited to terms of twelve years. This would not significantly reduce the average term of office of Successor Trustees, but it would permit the elections of younger men, who are often now passed over because the incumbent Successor Trustees do not want to commit a lifetime post to a young man.

- Enfranchisement of recent graduates—The present disenfranchisement of Yale College graduates for the first five years after their graduation should be terminated.

Several other improvements in the selection of trustees can be made, fortunately, without legislative action. The Commission consequently recommends:

- Diversification—The Successor Trustees and the alumni should seek to diversify their choices in the dimensions indicated. Choosing a young man or woman is one small possible way to diversify. Equally important is ethnic, socioeconomic, sexual, religious, occupational diversification, not in order to "represent" various social and economic groups but to bring a variety of minds to the Corporation. Diversification should also bring a few greatly distinguished intellectuals to the Corporation, as well as one or two foreigners into the Corporation in acknowledgment of Yale's position as one of the world's major universities. Moreover, trustees should not be drawn exclusively from Yale alumni.

[1] This corrects for students' greatly outnumbering faculty; it gives each group as a whole equal weight.

- Successor Trustee consultation with faculty and students—The Corporation's search for Successor Trustees should incorporate consultation in each case with a faculty-student committee.

- Alumni consultation with faculty and students—Similarly, the Standing Committee of the Alumni Board, in its search for nominees for alumni elections, should consult with a faculty-student committee to take advantage of the contribution that such a committee could make to its own search efforts.

- On procedures of the Corporation, the Commission recommends that: Appropriate committees of the Corporation should establish consulting relations with the newly proposed all-university advisory councils.

- Roughly once a month, perhaps on the occasion of meetings of the Corporation, two or three trustees should make themselves available for a limited time on campus to hear from any members of the Yale community who wish to bring proposals before them.

2. PRESIDENTS

Toronto:

That the initial term of office of the President, and each dean, chairman, and director be for up to five years. At the end of this period a committee similar to the one that recommended the initial appointment should consider all candidates for the position. If the incumbent is considered to be the most suitable person for the position, the term may be renewed once for a further period of up to five years.

American Academy of Arts and Sciences, Assembly on University Goals and Governance:

The college or university presidency is uniquely important in American higher education. The office needs to be strengthened so that it can more effectively fulfill its principal responsibilities. These are: to represent the general interest of the university as a whole; to be its spokesman; to be sensitive to the educational and intellectual needs and missions of the academic community; to be both a member of the faculty and its leader; to initiate major academic study and reform; to allocate resources to achieve specific educational goals and priorities. Together with the governing board, the president should plan for the development of the university (the planning process should involve all the constituencies to the fullest extent possible). Through the appointments the president makes to the administrative staff and those he or she influences in the professoriate, standards are set for integrity, educational achievement, vision and humanity. The president should perform his or her duties with as much grace, efficiency and absence of bureaucratic control as possible.

Princeton:

That at least one faculty representative from each Division of the University and at least one member of the non-tenured faculty participate in the deliberations of the committee elected to advise the Board of Trustees in any future search for a President of the University.

That representatives of the student body participate in consideration of candidates for President of the University.

That student and faculty members consulted by the Board of Trustees be elected by a procedure which will insure, insofar as that is possible, that they represent such diversity of opinion as may exist within the student body and the Faculty.

ACE:

Especially at the presidential level, responsibility must be accompanied by the necessary authority. Trustees, faculty, and students need to consider the possible ultimate consequence to them of weakening the president's authority. Institutions should have constitutions or bylaws which clearly define the responsibility *and* the authority of the president. In this connection, the nature of the presidency deserves rethinking. For example, fixed terms of office, renewable or unrenewable, might relieve some pressures on presidents, and also ensure institutional vitality. Fixed terms, or a system by which to review administrative tenure, might be preferable to the present system in which some presidents stay long beyond their real effectiveness or are sometimes sacrificed after one major incident. A division of authority—between "outside" concerns and "inside" ones, for example—might be considered where the burdens of the presidential office have grown too large for one man.

Presidents and other administrators have an especially urgent responsibility to ensure that avenues of communication are open. Some presidents are cut off by over-conscientious aides or secretaries; others are seldom seen on campus and never talk with students and seldom with faculty.

Harvard (*Supplementary Memorandum on the Choice of a New President: Term of Office and Review of Performance*, 1970):

It should be clearly understood, in the arrangement to be made by the Corporation with the next president that the maximum length of service contemplated (in the absence of extraordinary circumstances) should not exceed a period ranging between 10 and 14 years.

Beyond this specification, the Committee recommends that no predetermined fixed period of years should be established for the new president's term of office.

If the new president preferred an understanding with the Corporation that he would serve for a shorter term of, for example, five to seven years (with the possibility of renewal) then this option should not be precluded, so long as a maximum range of 10–14 years is kept in mind.

Rather than a narrow inquiry into the president's effectiveness, there should be a full-scale review of the state or progress of the University every four to eight years. The quality of the president's leadership would become apparent as the natural by-product of such a university-wide appraisal.

If change in the top leadership of the University were suggested by such a review, the governing boards should take whatever action the revealed circumstances suggested, regardless of original understandings about term of office. Options for appropriate reassignment should be sought to supplement the traditional alternatives of resignation, retirement, or dismissal.

Scranton Commission:

Administrators, principally the president, must bear most of the burden of defending the university against attacks from the outside and of articulating the university's needs and purposes to the public.

Because faculties are often wedded to the status quo, university administrators must provide much of the leadership for reform.

Above all, the administrator must keep open every possible channel of talk with students. He must have an open mind, for much that students say is valuable; he must have a cryptographer's mind, for much that they say comes in code words and postures; he must have an honest mind, for the worst crime in dealing with the young is to lie to them; he must have a tough mind, for he will frequently, for reasons either invisible or simply unintelligible to his hearers, have to say "No." Above all he must have a compassionate spirit—for youth is neither a disease nor a crime, though to its elders it may be one of the world's major puzzles.

3. FACULTY PARTICIPATION

Stanford:

The primary mechanism for faculty decision making on University-wide issues should be the Academic Senate acting either in its own right or through committees answerable to it.

Consecutive membership on a standing committee should be limited to two three-year terms. A person should be eligible for further appointment only after an absence from the committee of three years.

No person should serve as chairman of a faculty committee for more than three years.

An administrative officer whose area of operations falls within a committee's purview should participate in its deliberations without vote. He should be ineligible to serve as chairman.

Agenda and minutes of standing committees should be circulated to all relevant officers of administration, who should be entitled to attend and participate in any meeting in which they have an interest.

Standing committees should be provided with staff support. Chairmen of standing committees should receive relief from other duties commensurate with the obligations of their office.

Committees should be small enough to function effectively and to give each member a sense of responsibility for the committee's work. Only in exceptional circumstances should a committee number more than nine (inclusive of non-faculty members). Standing committees should be encouraged to form subcommittees some of whose members do not serve on the parent committee.

No faculty member should serve on more than one standing committee. In order to enforce that rule and to reduce scheduling problems, a special time should be set aside weekly for meetings of standing committees. This two-hour period should be kept free of scheduled classes and major campus events.

Toronto:

That the powers devolved by the Governing Council to the faculty level include the following:

a. curriculum planning;

b. admissions, student promotion, evaluation, degree-granting;

c. academic appointment, promotion, and tenure;

d. allocation of budget and resources granted by the Governing Council to the faculty;

e. student petitions and appeals, with provision for further appeal to the Governing Council.

American Academy of Arts and Sciences,
Assembly on University Goals
and Governance:

Arguments for representative faculty senates or for town-meeting faculty senates are legion. The small college can function well with the latter type. The larger institution should think seriously of having both—the representative body for most issues, the town-meeting senate when a sizable proportion of the faculty wishes an opportunity for further deliberation. Small groups of faculty generally dominate faculty senates and similar organizations. At many colleges and universities a large number of faculty either choose to avoid senate assignments or are not invited to take part in them. The same names appear repeatedly in the membership of key committees. If faculty self-governance is in fact to flourish, many who are devoted to teaching and scholarship, who would often rather staff aloof from administrative responsibilities, need to become involved. Membership in the executive bodies of large senates or in representative senates or major faculty committees ought to rotate.

Faculty or faculty-student committees have grown more important in the governance of colleges and universities. These are sometimes chosen by administrators, who have some sort of "representative" principle in mind. In other cases, they are chosen by senates, university councils, and similar groups. Departmental, divisional, school, and other committees have also proliferated. Committees in such profusion create confusion. Their number ought to be reduced and a time limit should often be set for them. To save the energies of both faculty and students, and to make committees more effective, the more important ones ought to have administrative staff members assigned to them. This, of course, raises the hazard of committees becoming the servants of the staff, but that problem can be guarded against, whereas the inefficiency that frequently develops when there is no staff cannot.

AAHE-NEA Task Force:
An evaluation of the essential functions of administrators and faculty leads to the judgment that an effective system of campus governance should be built on the concept of "shared authority" between the faculty and the administration.

A meaningful application of the concept of "shared authority" should involve a wide variety of issues. The issues include educational and administrative policies; personnel administration; economic matters ranging from the total resources available to the institution to the compensation for particular individuals; public questions that affect the role and functions of the institutions; and procedures for faculty representation in campus governance.

A further, broad distinction may be made between "aggregate" issues that affect the faculty as a whole and "individual" issues that have a special relevance for the individual faculty members.

There are various levels of decision-making for different issues in colleges and universities, especially those institutions in large public systems. Arrangements for faculty representation in campus governance must be related to the locus of decision-making in the institution and the system.

Several types of organizations can provide for faculty representation in campus governance:

An internal organization, such as the academic senate, is an integral part of the structure of the institution in which the faculty is represented.

An external association, such as the AAUP, attempts to exert influence outside of the framework of formal campus governance.

A bargaining agency, such as some locals of the American Federation of Teachers or some units and affiliates of the National Education Association, seeks to enter into formal negotiations with the administration with the objective of reaching a written agreement.

Faculty members should have the right to select the type of organization, or the combination of organizational arrangements, that they believe is most appropriate to their needs.

There are three alternative approaches of faculty-administration decision-making in campus governance. These include information-sharing and appeals to reason, the use of neutral third parties, and the application of political, educational, or economic sanctions. The greatest reliance should be placed on information-sharing and appeals of reason.

Neutral third-party intervention, such as arbitration, can be used constructively when an impasse arises between the faculty and the administration. Sanctions should be applied only where vital issues are involved and other methods of resolving disputes have failed. Although the strike is a weapon of last resort, there are no persuasive reasons to deny faculty members the right to use this sanction.

The concept of "shared authority" can best be implemented through the establishment of an internal organization, preferably an academic senate. An effective senate should meet the following requirements:

The senate which has decision-making authority normally should include both faculty members and administrators. Faculty members should comprise a clear majority of the senate.

The structure of the senate should take into account the structure of the institution in which it operates. This means that in states with comprehensive plans of higher education, the structure of the senate should be extended to multicampus units.

Most "aggregate" issues, affecting the faculty as a whole, should be decided by the senate. However, it is recognized that some issues, such as grading standards, should be primarily under faculty control, while other issues, such as the business management of the institution, should be primarily under the control of the administrators.

The senate should establish a special budget committee to deal with the general allocation of resources among the component parts and programs of the institution.

The senate should rely upon information-sharing and appeals to reason as the preferred approach to resolving faculty-administration disputes. Political and educational sanctions may be used in serious disputes that have not been resolved through other methods.

A formal appeals procedure should be established to resolve

disputes involving individual faculty members and the administration.

The substantive scope of the appeals procedure should be determined by the academic senate.

The appeals procedure may make provision for neutral third-party intervention, including arbitration.

External associations such as the American Association of University Professors and the American Association for Higher Education can act as a constructive complement to the academic senate by providing information and technical services, and by supporting educational sanctions if they should become necessary.

Scranton Commission:
Many faculty members know very little about the operation of their universities. They should inform themselves about the principles, mechanisms, and constraints that are involved in decision-making, rather than simply demand dramatic changes without demonstrating how they can be achieved.

Faculty committees should be established to evaluate and guide the teaching performance of faculty members.

Yale:
Officers of the University, deans, and department chairmen should make it a practice to include liberal representation of nontenured faculty on all policy committees, including departmental executive committees.

The President should consult nontenured faculty in the choice of their departmental chairmen.

In each school, the faculties should create a specific body, structure, or process that locates responsibility for significant educational reform in the hands of some of its faculty.

A proposal specific to Yale College is that the faculty establish a somewhat autonomous interdepartmental curriculum planning and teaching group. It could be charged with designing, and teaching where necessary, educational programs not now offered by existing departments or interdepartmental committees. Faculty in the new group would remain active in their own disciplines, and many of them would return wholly to their regular departments after a few years in the program. Such a group could develop new major programs, as well as four-year, three-year, and one-year programs. It could also experiment with sequences of courses of increasing intellectual challenge and other groups of courses, as well as individual courses. The point of such a proposal is to enlist a first-class segment of the faculty in a new commitment to teaching and educational work, to give them institutional support in their new commitment, and to put them in a strong position to exert educational leadership by both planning and actually teaching courses and programs.

4. COLLECTIVE BARGAINING

AAHE-NEA Task Force:

Formal bargaining relationships between the faculty and the administration are most likely to develop if the administration has failed to establish or support effective internal organizations for faculty representation. In such institutions, the faculty should have the right to choose a bargaining representative.

Bargaining agencies will tend to focus on economic matters, such as compensation, and issues of personnel administration. They will also press for a formal grievance procedure to handle disputes between individuals and the administration.

Even though a bargaining agency is present, certain "aggregate" issues of educational policy and administration may be assigned to an academic senate. However, the relationships between the bargaining agency and the senate probably will be highly unstable.

Bargaining agencies may develop and utilize decision-making techniques based on information-sharing and reason, but they may resort to sanctions, such as the strike, when crucial issues are at stake and other means have been exhausted. Although strikes are generally undesirable in institutions of higher education, under certain circumstances they may be a less destructive alternative than other sanctions.

Some system of faculty representation is likely to emerge in most institutions. The pattern of campus governance that prevails in the future will be determined by the measures that governing boards and administrators take to deal with faculty aspirations now.

5. FACULTY APPOINTMENT

Toronto:

That with respect to new appointments, the task of the personnel (or an ad hoc) committee in the department be to advertise the position, generate names, arrange for seminars, circulate curricula vitae of the candidates involved, and finally submit these names to the department chairman, in order of choice. The chairman has the responsibility for the final selection of the candidate for appointment and for negotiation of contract and salary.

Princeton:

That departmental chairmen regularly invite both graduate and undergraduate student departmental committees to attach comments to any requests for authorization to seek new staff positions (as these are defined in terms of academic specialties) being forwarded by their departments to the Dean of the Faculty.

That the Dean of the Faculty—working with the Dean of the College, the Committee on the Course of Study, and the Academic Committee of the Undergraduate Assembly—devise regular ways to make a limited number of extra-departmental appointments of limited term.

That the Administration seek to ascertain in a systematic way the views of non-tenured faculty members on the manner in which decisions on appointments and advancements are made in their departments.

Yale:

Where possible on original appointments and in any case for internal promotions, the documents supporting the request for favorable action on a candidate should include course outlines and bibliographies prepared by the candidate, as well as other documents, if any exist, representing the candidate's educational work. Systematic written student evaluations should also be included. This is, of course, in addition to the documents bearing on his research skills. The oral presentation to the appointments committee on the candidate's behalf should embrace not simply the usual summary judgment that he is an "excellent" or "good" teacher but specific points of information and appraisal bearing on the current competence with which the candidate has attacked his problems of course and curriculum design and other problems in teaching.

That the President should constitute a special standing search committee, acting for the faculty as a whole or perhaps for the Faculty of Arts and Sciences, with a continuing obligation to make special efforts to seek intellects and talents of extraordinary gifts and reach for the Yale faculty, preferably as permanent appointments but also as visitors.

6. FACULTY PROMOTION AND TENURE

Toronto:

That promotions not involving tenure and below the rank of full professor be made by the chairman of the department on the advice of the departmental personnel committee, meeting in two parts or collectively as its members choose.

That promotions to full professor and the award of tenure be made by the dean on the advice of an ad hoc personnel committee of the faculty council, meeting in two parts or collectively as its members choose.

That a common policy on promotion and tenure obtain throughout the university and that suitable committees to coordinate the decisions made in these areas by both university and college departments be established. Intercollegiate departments would, once more, be the simplest device to provide such coordination.

White House Conference on Youth:

A sensitive area of decision-making is that of promoting teachers and administrators to tenure on both the secondary and college level. The present system protects poor teachers and administrators and provides little stimulus for updating of skills and knowledge. The present system puts the burden of success solely on students and not on the ability of the teacher or administrator.

The teacher and administrator tenure system should be revamped. Since good teaching should be the criterion for tenure, teaching quality should be assessed on the basis of evaluations by students, colleagues who have observed the teacher, administrators, and the teacher himself. Teachers entering a system should be given the option of a one year contract or a limited tenure period. Renewal of contract should be based on cumulative evaluations.

Implementation: (1) Students should be provided the opportunity to evaluate the effectiveness of their teachers and administrators at least once a year. Evaluation from students along with evaluations from colleagues, administrators, community members and the teacher, himself, should be the basis for renewal of contract.

(2) Each school should establish a personnel committee composed of representatives from the student body, administration, faculty, and community to review the evaluations of each teacher and administrator and to make decisions concerning renewing or discontinuing a contract.

(3) Teachers and administrators should be hired for a maximum period of three years with renewal based on cumulative evaluations. The personnel committee of each school should make the decision to renew or withdraw a contract.

American Association of State Colleges and Universities:
Academic Freedom and Responsibility: Academic freedom is the right of members of the academic community freely to study, discuss, investigate, teach, conduct research, publish or administer as appropriate to their respective roles and responsibilities. It is the responsibility of administrators to protect and assure these rights within the governing framework of the institution. The teacher is entitled to freedom in the classroom in discussing his subject, but he should be careful to present the various scholarly views related to his subject and to avoid introducing into his teaching controversial or other matter which has no relation to his subject. The teacher is entitled to full freedom in research and in the publication of the results therefrom, subject to the adequate performance of his other academic duties.

However, academic freedom should be distinguished clearly from constitutional freedom, which all citizens enjoy equally under the law. Academic freedom is an additional assurance to those who teach and pursue knowledge, and, thus, properly should be restricted to rights of expression pertaining to teaching and research within their areas of recognized professional competencies. Beyond this, expressions by members of the academic community should carry no more weight or protection than that accorded any other citizen under the guarantee of constitutional rights: that is, outside of one's professional field, one must accept the same responsibility which all other individuals bear for their acts and utterances. In these cases, there is and should be no guaranteed immunity from possible criticism under the guise of academic freedom; however, when a member of the academic community speaks or writes as a citizen, he should be free from institutional censorship or discipline, but as a man of learning he should remember that the public may judge his profession and his institution by his utterances so he should at all times be accurate, should exercise appropriate restraint, should show respect for the opinions of others and should indicate that he is not an institutional spokesman.

The concept of academic freedom must be accompanied by an equally demanding concept of academic responsibility. The concern of the institution and its members for academic freedom safeguards must extend equally to requiring responsible service, consistent with the objectives of the institution.

Institutions of higher education are committed to open and rational discussion as a principal means for the clarification of issues and the solution of problems. In the solution of certain difficult problems, all members of the academic community must take note of their responsibility to society, to the institution, and to each other and must recognize that at times the interests of each may vary and will have to be reconciled. The use of physical force, psychological harassment, or other disruptive acts, which interfere with institutional activities, freedom of movement on the campus, or freedom of all members of the academic community to pursue their rightful goals, is the antithesis of academic freedom and responsibility. So, also, are acts which, in effect, deny freedom to speak, to be heard, to study, to teach, to administer and to pursue research. It is incumbent upon each member of the academic community to be acquainted with his individual responsibilities, as delineated by appropriate institutional statements.

The universal responsibility of the teaching faculty member is effective teaching. A proper academic climate can be maintained only when members of the academic community meet their fundamental responsibilities regularly, such as preparing for and meeting their assignments, conferring with and advising students, evaluating fairly and reporting promptly student achievement, and participating in group deliberations which contribute to the growth and development of students and the institution. All members of the academic community also have the responsibility to accept those reasonable duties assigned to them within their fields of competency, whether curricular, co-curricular or extra-curricular. Additionally, the concept of "institutional loyalty" still has a proper place within the academic community and imposes the further responsibility on all members of the academic community to attempt, honestly and in good faith, to preserve and defend the institution and the goals it espouses, without restricting the right to advocate change.

Administrators must protect, defend and promote academic freedom, must assure that members of the academic community fulfill their responsibilities, and, in addition, must recognize that they have special responsibilities for which they are held accountable—namely, the marshaling of human, physical and financial resources in order to realize institutional goals.

Academic Tenure: The traditional protection afforded by tenure against unwarranted dismissal of teachers has its validity today as in the past. Tenure is not, nor should it be intended as, however, a shield for mediocrity, incompetence, or academic irresponsibility, and faculties at each institution should clearly and explicitly establish minimum levels of expected professional performance and responsibility and should enforce them impartially.

Those institutions which provide for academic tenure should have clear statements in their regulations as to the conditions, including due process, that must be met for tenure to be awarded and continued and for appointments to be terminated.

Academic tenure is not prerequisite to academic freedom, for academic freedom is the right of all members of the academic community as is responsibility the obligation of all. Rather, tenure, where recognized, is a specific provision of employment which is accorded to those members of the academic community who qualify for it, is a means of making the teaching profession attractive to persons of ability, and constitutes one important protection for academic freedom. It, thus, contributes to the success of an institution in fulfilling its obligations to its students and to society.

American Academy of Arts and Sciences, Assembly on University Goals and Governance:
Appointment to permanent tenure is often regarded as the most important stage in an academic career. Colleges and universities are derelict when they make the most searching inquiry to determine whether an individual merits a permanent post and

do nothing to encourage creativity once the person is installed in that post. The intellectual growth of its faculty ought to be a prime responsibility of any institution concerned with the intellectual growth of its students. Colleagueship will have a determining influence in this matter. So, also, will the administrative decisions that grant time to individual faculty members, not as sabbaticals and not tied to specific projects financed from outside, but as an opportunity to explore new areas relevant to their teaching and research. To make these decisions wisely, deans and presidents will need to inform themselves more thoroughly about the teaching and scholarly contributions of professors.

In many institutions, an initial appointment carries the presumption of the right of re-appointment. Tenure is generally automatic in such instances on re-appointment after a number of years of service. The growth of unionization and collective bargaining reinforce this practice and also reinforce the practice of having uniform salary scales. The principle of differential rewards for merit in teaching and scholarship, which exists for very good reasons, should not be tampered with where it still prevails.

There is little self-regulation by faculty in most institutions. Only the most flagrant evidence of gross misbehavior will involve an individual in disciplinary actions initiated by colleagues. Desirably, the faculty member who, for example, interferes with the academic freedoms of colleagues or students ought to be subject to faculty-imposed sanctions under a self-generated code of faculty conduct and responsibility. The alternative to such self-regulation may be a form of additional outside control that carries hazards for intellectual freedom in the colleges and universities of the country.

Despite the abuses common to permanent positions, professorial tenure needs to be retained as a guarantor of academic freedom against political and other pressures. Yet, means ought to be developed to encourage and facilitate the early departure of those who are making small contributions to their institution and their students. To this end, pensions should be reorganized so that professors may retire (and in some cases be encouraged to retire) at substantial partial pay after twenty years of tenured service at one or more universities. This arrangement is similar to others that prevail in the foreign service, the military and various civil service systems where indemnity offers a viable reconciliation between competence and security.

When a professor retires, resigns, or dies, it is generally assumed that the vacancy in the field will be automatically filled. This is an unwise policy, since it prevents response to new priorities unless the institution grows in size. Every vacancy ought to revert to a campus-wide pool where the requirements for a particular specialism can be weighed by administrators and faculty against requirements for other fields.

ACE:

Tenure policies—concerning a faculty member's right to hold his academic appointment until retirement once competence has been demonstrated (except when extreme malfeasance has been established by due process)—need to be reappraised. The justification for tenure is the crucial protection it gives to academic freedom. Professors who espouse unpopular views must be free from reprisal. Tenure was not devised in the spirit of trade union systems to guarantee job security. But it has come to serve this function too, at a cost. It sometimes has been a shield for indifference and neglect of scholarly duties. At a time when an increasing number of teachers, especially in community colleges and state colleges, are organizing for collective bargaining, the Committee recognizes that a challenge to the present concept of tenure is no small matter, that the issues involved are complex and difficult to resolve, and that a satisfactory solution must maintain effective safeguards for academic freedom. Nonetheless, we urge the American Association of University Professors and the Association of American Colleges (co-sponsors of the basic 1940 Statement on Academic Freedom and Tenure) to join with representatives of other educational organizations that are concerned with tenure, including the American Federation of Teachers, the National Student Association, and constituents of the American Council on Education, to reexamine existing policies. Standards for awarding tenure—a matter of institutional autonomy—need broadening to allow greater consideration of teaching ability. Scholarly communities must be protected as effectively as tenure now protects individual professors.

Scranton Commission:

As one means of improving the quality of teaching in higher education, we urge reconsideration of the practice of tenure. Tenure has strong justifications because of its role in protecting the academic freedom of senior faculty members. But it also can protect practices that detract from the institution's primary functions, that are unjust to students, and that grant faculty members a freedom from accountability that would be unacceptable for any other profession.

Yale:

Within the Faculty of Arts and Sciences, departments intending not to renew a faculty appointment should, through the chairman of the relevant appointments committee, notify the committee of its intention. The committee can, then, if it wishes, ask the department to defend its action, if the concerned faculty member does not object.

Utah:

The tenure system at the University of Utah should be maintained. Affirmative measures should be undertaken by the University Community to assure full compliance by all faculty members with professional standards of performance and responsibility.

The University community should initiate appropriate proceedings leading to the adoption of a Code of Faculty Responsibilities, consistent with traditionally accepted principles of academic freedom.

Association of American Colleges:

The 1940 "Statement of Principles on Academic Freedom and Tenure," which was co-sponsored and endorsed by the Association of American Colleges, recognizes that an institution may find it necessary to curtail or eliminate an academic program for reasons of financial exigency. Such program retrenchment may require termination of probationary and/or tenured faculty members of the faculty. The 1940 Statement, which applies only to tenured faculty, provides in this regard that "termination of a continuous appointment because of financial exigency should be demonstrably bona fide."

The principles and procedures stated below are commended to institutions facing the necessity of curtailing educational programs and terminating tenured or probationary staff appointments.

A college or university must dedicate all of its resources to the greatest possible achievement of its educational goals and purposes. Fiscal policy should reflect this commitment. In meeting this commitment unfavorable economic conditions may require an institution to reevaluate its priorities and reallocate limited financial resources. When it becomes necessary to curtail or eliminate some educational programs and terminate some staff appointments, the importance of such decisions to an institution, its students, and the members of its academic staff requires the closest possible coordination of fiscal and academic planning. In particular, fair and effective procedures should be designed, if possible, before a crisis develops.[1]

In situations where curtailment or elimination of educational programs may be necessary for reasons of financial exigency the following guidelines may be useful:

1 *Consultation.*   Early in the process of making recommendations or decisions concerning program reduction, administrators and faculty policy groups should consult widely with their colleagues, students, and others in the college community. It is especially important that faculty members whose educational programs or positions may be adversely affected have an opportunity to be heard by those who will make the final decision or recommendation.

2 *Data and Documentation.*   Every effort must be made to determine the nature of the fiscal limitations and within those constraints to establish appropriate educational priorities. Careful documentation of the evidence supporting a staff reduction decision is essential. Appropriate financial information, student-faculty ratios, qualitative program and course evaluations, enrollment data, and other pertinent information should be used to support a case of financial exigency. Except for con-

---

[1] It is recommended that institutions inform all faculty appointees in writing at the time of their initial employment of the conditions under which appointments may be terminated for reasons of financial exigency.

fidential material of a personal nature this information should be widely shared among the college community.

3 *Timing.* Institutions should provide as much lead time as possible in making financial exigency decisions. In cases where faculty appointments are to be terminated timely notice of termination or nonreappointment must be given.[2] In extreme situations, if timely notice cannot be given, financial compensation to the faculty member proportional to the lateness of the notice may be an appropriate substitute for full notice.

4 *Academic Due Process.* When program reductions in response to financial exigency involve termination of faculty appointments special care must be taken to insure fairness and to protect and honor accepted procedures and rights appropriate to a faculty member's tenured or probationary status.[3] Faculty members must have an opportunity to be heard by those who will make the staff reduction decisions and those decisions must be subject to review by the highest institutional authority. Care should be taken not to confuse termination because of financial exigency with a proceeding that might lead to dismissal for cause.[4]

5 *Elimination of a Faculty Position.* If an appointment is terminated before the end of the period of appointment, because of financial exigency, or because of the discontinuance of a pro-

[2] Although not formally endorsed by AAC, the AAUP 'Standards of Notice for Nonreappointment' have been widely accepted by the academic community. (*AAUP Bulletin*, Winter 1967, vol. 53, no. 4, p. 407).

[3] In this regard consult the AAUP "1968 Recommended Institutional Regulations on Academic Freedom and Tenure," paragraph 4c, *AAUP Bulletin*, Vol. 54, No. 4., Winter 1968, pp. 448–452, and "Procedural Standards in the Renewal and Nonrenewal of Faculty Appointments," *AAUP Bulletin*, Summer 1971, Vol. 57, No. 2, pp. 206–210. These AAUP policy statements have not been formally endorsed by AAC.

[4] There may be some temptation to seize upon financial exigency as an occasion to remove an allegedly incompetent staff member. In the latter case the appropriate proceeding is a dismissal hearing and the faculty member is entitled to the protections and standards of due process set forth in the 1940 "Statement of Principles on Academic Freedom and Tenure," *Association of American Colleges Bulletin*, March 1941, Vol. 27, No. 1, pp. 127–129, or *AAUP Bulletin*, Autumn 1970, Vol. 56, No. 3, pp. 323–326, and the "Statement on Procedural Standards in Faculty Dismissal Proceedings," *Association of American Colleges Bulletin*, March 1958, Vol. 44, No. 1, pp. 125–130, or *AAUP Bulletin*, Winter 1968, Vol. 54, No. 4, pp. 439–441. Both of these statements have been endorsed by AAC.

gram of instruction, the released faculty member's place will not be filled by a replacement within a period of two years, unless the released faculty member has been offered reappointment and a reasonable time within which to accept or decline it.[5]

6 *Preferential Treatment.* Tenured members of the faculty should normally be retained in preference to probationary appointees. This preferential status should include wherever possible an opportunity to transfer or readapt to other programs within the department or institution. If retention is not possible the institution should assume responsibility for assisting the faculty member in securing other employment. Preferential retention of tenured faculty should not, however, leave a reduced academic unit in the highly undesirable situation of lacking any probationary faculty. In some cases, tenured and probationary faculty may both have to be reduced.[6]

7 *Alternatives.* Early retirement and transfer from full-time to part-time service may be acceptable alternatives to termination in some situations of financial exigency. However, such decisions should be governed by the same guidelines and procedural safeguards as those which result in termination.

---

[5] The language of this paragraph parallels that of the AAUP 1968 Recommended Institutional Regulations on Academic Freedom and Tenure (see footnote 8).

[6] Other considerations may also be germane in planning reductions which would force the institution to contradict its own goals and priorities or bring it into conflict with public policy. Strict adherence to preferential retention of tenured faculty members or strict recognition of seniority, for example, may result in disparate rates of reduction for women or members of ethnic and racial minorities and thus jeopardize recent progress toward fairer representation of these groups in the academic community. Staff reduction may also raise problems in relation to laws and regulations governing discrimination.

7. STUDENT PARTICIPATION

Stanford:

An appropriate number of students, as determined by the [Academic] Senate, should be members of the Senate without vote. These students should include the President and Vice-President of ASSU *ex officio* [Associated Students of Stanford University]. Additional student members should be elected in the spring general election of ASSU.

It should be presumed, in the absence of good cause shown to the contrary, that students have a contribution to make to the work of each University-wide, school, and departmental committee and therefore should be eligible for membership on each such committee. This eligibility should not extend to committees dealing with the appointment and promotion of faculty members. Students' judgment about the educational effectiveness of faculty members is valuable and should be used in reaching decisions of appointment and promotion.

The appropriate number of students on such committees should be determined in the case of committees of the Academic Council by the Senate's Committee on Committees and in the case of school and departmental committees by the faculties of the schools and departments.

The ASSU [Associated Students of Stanford University] should provide definite mechanisms for selecting student members of University committees in such a way that the opportunity to be considered for service is open to all and that adequate representation of various viewpoints is assured. As long as such mechanisms function, the selection of student members for committees of the Academic Council should be the exclusive responsibility of the ASSU. Similar principles should govern the selection of student members for school and department committees.

Toronto:

That there be a clearly established governing body for each department, centre, and institute. This body would be known as a council.

That, as soon as possible, departments set the required qualification for students to vote for representatives on the department council and to run for membership on the department council. These requirements should be set in consultation with the student union or club in these departments, if such—or similar—organizations exist, and must be ratified by the faculty council.

That, where the objectives of [the previous] recommendation cannot be achieved expeditiously by reliance on departmental mechanisms, the student and faculty members of a department, centre, or institute be defined by the council of the faculty or school of which the unit is a part. We would urge that this be done as soon as possible.

That the students in every department form a department students' union or club, and that this body be recognized as the legitimate representative voice of the students in any given department.

That negotiations be held between student and faculty members of the department to decide upon the proportions of representation on the department council and its committees, the negotiating committee to be made up of equal numbers of staff and students from the department. That negotiations be based on the parallel structures model, i.e. any agreement must be approved—separately and by majority vote—by both the staff and the members of the students' union or club before it can take effect.

That student unions have the right to define the extent to which their members on the department council and its committees are responsible to the student constituency as a whole.

That a method of recall be established which would enable students in a department to remove those of their representatives who were not acting according to the guidelines set up to govern the conduct of student members on the department council and its committees.

That, if an impasse is arrived at in the negotiation for the composition of the department council and its committees, the dean of the faculty, in consultation with the negotiation committee, appoint a mediator or small mediation committee acceptable to both students and staff of the department. The mediators shall exert their best efforts to bring the staff and students to an agreement.

That, if mediation carried out as in [the previous] recommendation should fail, the composition of the department council and its committees be fixed by an ad hoc committee of the Governing Council, this committee to consist of two staff members chosen by the faculty representatives on the Governing Council, two student members chosen by the student representatives on the Council, a layman chosen by these four, and the President serving as non-voting chairman.

That properly conducted elections to the department council be held once a year. The right of election of faculty members to the council should not be based on rank or seniority. Adequate representation from both graduate and undergraduate student constituencies should be ensured.

That department councils may invite persons other than their own faculty and students to join them or their committees. These persons might be from other departments, from the departmental support staff, from the graduates, from professional associations, from licensing bodies, or from secondary schools, etc.

That the department council have the functions of making policy, advising the executive and reviewing the implementation of all policy matters within the jurisdiction of the department. This would include policy on personnel, curriculum, budget allocation, research and consulting, short-range and long-range planning, space allocation, teaching methods, non-academic staff, and other appropriate matters.

That, where feasible, department councils be unitary, i.e. that both graduate and undergraduate staff and students be included in their membership and that such councils have responsibility for both the graduate and undergraduate policies of the department.

That any part of the university which administers its own degree or diploma programme be known as a faculty. That the term "division" be reserved for a section of a faculty.

That, where feasible, all faculty councils consist of academic staff, students and administrators. That the proportion of representation of these three groups be as follows:

- Academic Staff $^2/_5$—two-fifths
- Students $^2/_5$—two-fifths
- Administrators $^1/_5$—one-fifth

That the size of faculty councils generally not exceed one hundred.

That all elections to faculty councils be on a constituency basis, so that staff and students may be fairly represented on council. That part-time staff, because their affiliation with the university may be minimal, have only a small representation, to be decided upon by the faculty council.

That meetings of the faculty council and its committees generally be open.

That others (e.g. graduates, support staff, and secondary schools) be invited to send representatives to faculty councils.

That any student registered in the faculty be eligible for membership on the faculty council and to vote in elections to faculty council.

That any member of the full-time staff be eligible for membership on council and to vote in elections to faculty council.

That the student representation from each division on the graduate faculty council be made equal to the academic staff representation from each division.

That, where necessary, each graduate department council be formed according to the principles outlined for undergraduate departments.

White House Conference on Youth:
America's democratic system is rooted in the belief that all citizens who are affected by the system should have a voice in deciding how the system is to be set up. This concept of a representative democracy has not been universally accepted in our Nation's educational institutions. As students on all levels become increasingly socially and politically aware, the time has come to give students a voice in the policy and governance of their educational system.

To facilitate education, students must be thought of as participants, not merely recipients of the educational process.

Beginning with the secondary level, students should participate in educational decisions and student governance. They should also participate in broad-based policy decisions by having representatives on educational and governing boards at all levels and in governmental agencies. Special efforts must be made to include racial and ethnic minorities, students in vocational and non-academic concentrations, and other students who, for various reasons, traditionally tend not to be involved in educational governance. As members of the community, they should be indispensable participants in sound decision-making. In those instances where students are not voting members, steps should be taken to move toward giving them voting representation.

Institutions of Higher Education: (1) Policy making bodies in institutions of higher education should include students as voting members. Every institution should have clearly defined procedures, voted on by the total academic community, for selecting members of bodies which make and implement policy.

The procedures for selection of these students should reflect all aspects of the student community. Also, for truly effective participation, provisions should be made for terms of more than one year. Where financial need might prevent a student from participating, procedures should be established to provide the needed assistance.

Opportunities to earn course credit for involvement in university governance should be provided for student members.

Students should take seriously their obligation to participate when there are opportunities for real influence on policy. Some examples of areas in which students are seeking such a voice are recommendations on tenure and promotion, curriculum, grading reform, and course and faculty evaluation.

Student participation and full membership is needed not only on top level policy making and governing boards, but also on commissions, councils, and working committees throughout the educational system.

American Academy of Arts and Sciences, Assembly on University Goals and Governance:
Examination of prevailing extra-curricular activities suggests that many were created in the nineteenth century to assist adolescent boys to enjoy collegial living. Faculty and other adult supervision was provided as a way of showing the institution's concern for its charges. Colleges and universities would be well-advised to reconsider their commitment to support such

extra-curricular pursuits. If students, increasingly adult, are to be independent, they must choose those activities they wish to maintain and must consider how to support them. There may be a sound educational reason for the extra-curriculum being placed wholly in the hands of students at certain institutions, making possible experiments of a kind that cannot be expected to originate in the votes of faculties or governing boards. At certain other institutions, where the extra-curriculum is seen as an integral part of the educational experience, almost indistinguishable from the curriculum, faculties may choose to exercise greater leadership.

Student government is a misnomer in almost all institutions. It rarely governs, though it often provides a forum where student views on the governing of colleges and universities are heard. The centralization of student politics, a result of having a student government, may reduce the involvement of students in the decentralized schools and departments of the institution. When this happens it is unfortunate, because the greatest possibility of students influencing educational policy can occur on a decentralized basis. This is the kind of student involvement that should be fostered.

Many activities in addition to the extra-curricular ones now handled by students might desirably be delegated to them. For example, on some campuses the responsibility for residence halls and other living arrangements ought to rest with students, as is the case in several European countries. These, and similar experiments, should be monitored; it is possible that some functions can be better performed by students than by others

Princeton:

Undergraduate Students: That student departmental committees and departmental chairmen be jointly responsible for adopting procedures for the election of student departmental committees that have these objectives:

- It should be convenient for the students of the department to vote.

- There should be an opportunity for any departmental student to place names in nomination.

- It should be easy for relatively small groups of students to have a representative on their department's committee and difficult for an organized minority to capture a disproportionate share of committee positions.

- There should be reasonable precautions against multiple balloting and reasonable measures to insure a fair count of the vote.

That departmental chairmen be responsible for:

- Referring all proposals for changes in departmental undergraduate programs to their student committees before action on such proposals is taken by departmental faculties.

- Inviting members of student committees to discuss proposals for changes in departmental undergraduate programs with departmental faculties at or before any meetings in which departmental faculties take action on such proposals.

- Scheduling at least two meetings each academic year with their student committees, one early in the fall term to work out plans for later consultation, and one in late spring to review departmental undergraduate offerings so that chairmen may take student views into account in preparing requests for new staff.

That student committees and faculty departmental committees concerned with the undergraduate program (in departments in which the latter sort of committee exists) normally meet jointly.

That student departmental committees have the following additional prerogatives:

- The right to attach comments, favorable or unfavorable, to all proposals forwarded by the faculties of their departments to the Committee on the Course of Study.

- A reasonable amount of secretarial and other assistance in preparing proposals, communicating with departmental majors, and conducting elections.

- The right in certain circumstances to secure a departmental faculty's reconsideration of action taken on proposals regarding the course of study for undergraduate students. Specifically: Departmental faculties should seriously consider a second vote on any measure regarding the department's undergraduate program, when a second vote is requested by the student committee of the department. In any particular academic year departmental faculties should commit themselves to a second vote on such measures if a second vote is requested within one month by the student committee in a petition endorsed by two-thirds of the department's majors. If the action being reconsidered is on a proposal that the departmental faculty has rejected, a majority vote of the departmental faculty should reverse the previous decision. If the action being reconsidered is on a proposal that has been adopted by the departmental faculty, a two-thirds vote of the departmental faculty should be required to affirm the previous decision. Departmental faculties should not be bound to reconsider the same action more than once in the same academic year.

That the Academic Committee of the Undergraduate Assembly, or a subcommittee thereof, normally meet jointly with the Faculty Committee on the Course of Study, so long as the student committee remains at about its present size (5 members). Student members of the UGA Committee . . . shall have the right to attach comments to any proposals forwarded to the Faculty by the Committee on the Course of Study and to appear at meetings of the Faculty to present the views of the student committee on such proposals.

That the Dean of Students seek the advice of the Undergraduate Assembly regarding the allocation of grants-in-aid to organizations of undergraduate students.

That the Dean of Students and the Dean of the College (or their representatives) regularly attend meetings of the Undergraduate Assembly to report, and answer questions about, the current and prospective activities of their Offices.

That the Offices of the Dean of Students and the Dean of the College provide a reasonable amount of clerical assistance to the Undergraduate Assembly and its Committees on the Course of Study and Undergraduate Life.

Graduate Students: That each department establish a departmental committee of graduate students, to act as a liaison between the faculty and the graduate student body of the department. Each committee should normally meet with the committee of the departmental faculty concerned with graduate studies, if one exists. The committee of graduate students should have the right to initiate discussion of any proposals relating to the departmental graduate program, should encourage students to participate in departmental affairs of special interest and relevance to them, and should have the following additional prerogatives:

[Editorial note: Same prerogatives as those listed above for undergraduate committees.]

That each departmental chairman be responsible for:

- Referring all proposals for changes in his department's graduate program to the departmental graduate student committee before action on such proposals by the faculty of his department.

- Inviting student committee members to discuss proposals for changes in the graduate course of study with the faculty of his department at or before any meetings in which the departmental faculty proposes to take action on such proposals.

- Scheduling at least two meetings each academic year with the graduate student committee of his department, one early in the fall term to work out plans for later consultation, and one in late spring to review the department's graduate offerings so that chairmen may take student views into account in preparing requests for new staff.

That a properly constituted, University-wide organization of graduate students have the right to attach comments to proposals regarding the graduate course of study being forwarded to the Faculty, the right to send representatives to meetings of the Faculty to speak for or against such proposals, and the right, upon a two-thirds vote of its members, to obtain a second vote by the Faculty on any decision about the graduate curriculum. The Faculty would not be bound, however, to reconsider the same action more than once in the same academic year.

That a University-wide body of graduate students be established to serve as a forum for expression of opinion on matters of interest to graduate students and to represent the views of graduate students to other bodies in the University and to the University's administrative officers; that such a body include one member from each of the academic departments and two members from each of the residentially based committees of graduate students; and that any quasi-legislative functions be assumed by such a body only with the consent of the graduate student body as a whole.

That the Council of the Princeton University Community, the Faculty, the officers of the University satisfy themselves that such an organization of graduate students is properly constituted before delegating quasi-legislative authority to it.

ACE:

Students not only should be given substantial autonomy in their non-academic activities, but should also participate in matters of general educational policy, especially in curricular affairs. Since increased participation will contribute to effective institutional decision making and is also of educational benefit, students should serve in a variety of roles on committees that make decisions or recommendations. In some non-academic areas students should have effective control; in some general educational policy matters they should have voting participation; in other matters, they should act in an advisory or consultative capacity. Effective student representation will not only improve the quality of decisions; it will also help to ensure their acceptability to the student body.

As institutions give up policies of *in loco parentis* in response to students' educationally valid wishes for independence, students must know that they cannot be effectively shielded from the consequences of their behavior, especially when it violates the laws of society at large. The abandonment of parietal rules, however, does not relieve institutions of the need to have effective self-government. The more effective the self-government, the less frequently and abrasively will police and other agencies of the society intrude on the campus.

Students who want to propose changes in institutional practices or policies (as differentiated from asking redress of particular grievances) should be given the opportunity to learn in advance the institution's decision-making process that applies to their proposal. They should also consider thoroughly the evidence and arguments supporting their proposal and anticipate questions that will be raised by others, including fellow students. A well-considered proposal often grows out of preliminary discussion with faculty and administrators.

Students rightly expect administrators to exercise leadership, to take the initiative in proposing educational changes suited to a changing clientele and a changing society. But just as students are entitled to acceptance of their rights and responsibilities, so are administrators. Students should recognize that the administrator is responsible to widely divergent campus groups and is accountable to the board which legally governs the institution. Within these limitations, he must have freedom to initiate, guide, negotiate, and make decisions, if the institution is not to remain static. Attempts to circumscribe this freedom will either reinforce the status quo or create chaos.

Scranton Commission:
Increased participation of students, faculty, and staff in the formulation of university policies is desirable.

However, universities are not institutions that can be run on a one man, one vote basis or with the participation of all members on all issues.

Competence should be a major criterion in determining involvement in the university decision-making process.

Another criterion for involvement in decision-making should be the degree to which decisions affect any given group. Changes in regulations concerning student life should be made with the involvement of students; changes in faculty policies should obviously be made with faculty involvement.

Procedures for electing representatives of university constituencies should be carefully designed to guarantee true representativeness, perhaps by having representatives elected by small departmental or residential units, or by establishing quorum requirements to encourage participation and to enhance the legitimacy of the election result.

Reforms of governance should not undermine administrative leadership. On the contrary, they should be designed to produce policies and leaders who will have the broad support of the community, especially in times of campus crisis.

Once basic policy decisions are made, their execution should be left to expert administrative hands. Administrators must, of course, remain ultimately accountable to the various constituencies of the university—trustees, students, faculty, alumni, and the general public. But their actions should not be constantly overseen by any of these groups. The involvement of nonadministrators in the daily operations and minor policy decisions of the university erodes the effectiveness and sense of responsibility of administrators.

Yale:
All school and departmental faculties should put student

members on permanent or ad hoc curriculum or course of study committees and other permanent or ad hoc committees on educational issues (except for faculty appointments). Student membership on faculty committees is generally preferable to parallel committees.

As is now the practice in Yale College, school faculties should permit a student member of a school faculty committee to be present at a faculty meeting for the purpose of explaining his committee's reports.

For some purposes faculty should be able to meet without any students present and students should not vote in faculty meetings.

Whether students on departmental committees should attend departmental faculty meetings to present committee reports should be determined by each department.

The Corporation should arrange for a sample of students (or student representatives) of all schools to be systematically consulted in the selection of the University President. The President should systematically consult students in a school in the selection of its dean; and deans of schools and departmental chairmen should consult students in a department or school on the selection of a director of graduate studies or comparable official in a professional school.

British Joint Statement:
Student Participation in University Decision-Making: It was generally accepted that the problem of how students can make their views effectively felt within the decision-making processes in an individual university is not a simple one. Constitutionally, the power to make decisions in a university is widely dispersed. Most of the charters and statutes under which the universities operate, though differing from one another a good deal in detail, are in part guarantees of intellectual freedom and independence, and in part careful allocations of responsibility among the various elements of the university. The resulting structure may be complex, and the students recognize that in view of the fact that the period during which they can play an effective role in university government is limited, it is important that they should inform themselves fully and at an early

stage of the directions and manner in which their influence can be most effectively applied.

The National Union of Students seeks effective student presence on all relevant committees. Our discussions identified three broad areas of operation of such committees: (a) the whole field of student welfare—for example health services, catering facilities and the provision of accommodation—where there should in our view be varying degrees of participation of students in the decision-making process. Apart from this, there is the area which covers for example the operation of student unions and the management of a wide range of extra-curricular activities, in which most university student organisations rightly have long had complete responsibility; (b) that relating for example to curriculum and courses, teaching methods, major organisational matters, and issues concerning the planning and development of the university—where the ultimate decision must be that of the statutorily responsible body. In this area, we would regard it as essential that students' views should be properly taken into account; and (c) that involving for example decisions on appointments, promotions and other matters affecting the personal position of members of staff, the admissions of individuals and their academic assessment—where student presence would be inappropriate. Students should, however, have opportunities to discuss the general principles involved in such decisions and have their views properly considered.

. . . The machinery of student participation can and should be extended and improved. The means of doing this are likely to vary from one university to another. In those few cases where there is student membership of council or even in effect of senate, these will be watched with interest. The National Union of Students itself seeks student representation on these bodies. Frequently there is student membership of committees of council and of senate, and in the view of both parties there is scope for these practices to be extended. Not as an alternative but to supplement this we would welcome the development of joint staff-student committees in new and more effective forms, with substantial student membership and with a status equivalent to that of other committees of senate and council. These joint committees may operate not only at university level, but also, where appropriate, at faculty and departmental levels. We are agreed, however, that if such committees are to work well, the rules under which they operate must be the same as those which apply to any other university committee. All members must be on terms of equality, serving as representatives and not as delegates specifically mandated by the body which nominated them. They should be free to exercise their individual judgements in the light of committee discussion and be identified with its corporate decisions. If a recommendation of such a committee is not accepted, or is referred back by the parent body, the committee must be satisfied that its arguments were properly presented to that body and be informed of the reasons for their rejection.

All such measures of student participation depend for their effectiveness on the willingness of students to take part on these lines. When all facets of university life are taken into account, the numbers of students called upon to participate become quite large. They should, we believe, be student representatives in the real sense, understanding student needs and in sympathy with the aspirations of their fellow students. If the student organisations continue to be able to find representatives from a wide range of interest groups (e.g., departments, societies, etc.) and in the necessary numbers, we have no doubt their influence in the universities will continue to increase . . . .

Course Content and Teaching Methods: Discussion in this area must necessarily be subject to the clear right of the individual teacher, in consultation with his colleagues who by their scholarship in the relevant field of study have proved their right to an opinion, to decide on the way in which he presents his subject. Once this right is infringed from whatever quarter, from public pressure, from university governing bodies or from students themselves, the way is open to censorship and interference of every kind. We believe that the great majority of students are fully aware of the need to preserve this most essential of all academic freedoms. But we think that without any interference with this principle, it is possible and indeed right that there should be opportunities for students to enter into discussion about the content and structure of courses, about teaching methods in general, and about the effectiveness of the particular teaching which they are receiving. In general, the larger the university administrative division concerned, the more necessary it becomes that such opportunities should be offered through official committees at the appropriate levels.

It is often said that academic courses should "reflect the needs of society." A university should not only "reflect" current ideas and aspirations, but it must also subject these to rigorous intellectual analysis. It also has obligations to future needs both nationally and internationally. Clearly, where appropriate, the relevance of the subject in hand to the contemporary situation and to contemporary problems should be made explicit, but this we think is generally accepted as a prerequisite of good teaching at university level.

8. STUDENT EVALUATION OF FACULTY

Toronto:

That appropriate standard rating questionnaires be developed and administered routinely every year for all courses and teachers, so that broadly-based objective information is generated. These evaluations should be run by the student organizations in the department or faculty. Administrative and clerical assistance should be provided by the department or faculty office.

That retrospective evaluations on courses and teachers, to be obtained from graduating students, be organized by the student organizations in the department or faculty, with the administrative and clerical assistance of the department or faculty office.

American Academy of Arts and Sciences, Assembly on University Goals and Governance:

Teaching is still too little valued in too many colleges and universities. More systematic appraisal methods need to be introduced to identify and reward successful teachers. Student opinion in these matters is crucial, even though decisions on appointment ought to continue to rest with faculty and administration. Those who secure the benefits of good teaching—the students—ought to be included among the principal guardians of the teaching function. The hazard that such guardianship will encourage and favor showmanship and a quest for popularity can be overcome by policies that balance student preferences with the judgments of others, including colleagues. These judgments should include an estimate of the individual's capacity to attract able students, however few, and the importance of preserving specific fields whether or not they attract many students.

Princeton:

That the Dean of the Graduate School be responsible for developing procedures to survey the views of graduate students on the quality of their instruction.

ACE:

Effective teaching deserves greater recognition in hiring,

promoting, and paying, especially in the major institutions. Explicit methods must be developed for assessing teaching competence, improving the learning process, and systematically reviewing the adequacy of the curriculum. Quality of teaching must be given greater weight in tenure decisions. Faculty scholarship, research, and public service should relate more closely to teaching; indeed, they can enhance teaching. Both individual institutions and national professional organizations should establish fitting rewards for exceptional teachers. The Committee urges the learned and professional societies to explore other ways of giving more status to teaching and improving its quality, especially at the undergraduate level.

In matters affecting teaching—e.g., new faculty appointments; the awarding of tenure; new courses, departments, or interdisciplinary arrangements—faculty committees should seek the counsel of students who have had direct experience with the matter to be decided. The faculty, by virtue of its earned competence, is in the best position to have main jurisdiction over academic matters. But students, as the consumers of higher education and as young people with important perceptions about our changing society, have a right to be heard on matters affecting the educational program. As was pointed out in an earlier recommendation, participation by students could strengthen the quality of the decisions made and help to ensure their acceptability to the student body. In this connection, faculty should welcome the development by student organizations of formalized and objective procedures for evaluating faculty teaching of undergraduates in all important courses. Too often, student evaluations of teaching are fragmentary and are not available to the teacher, who might improve his teaching if he were aware of students' criticisms.

Scranton Commission:
At all levels of the university, excellence in teaching should be recognized, along with excellence in scholarly work, as a criterion for hiring, salary increases, and promotion. In the case of nontenured faculty, clear evaluation procedures emphasizing both teaching and research should be developed, publicized, and used.

Students should be provided with regular means for evaluating courses and the teaching effectiveness of faculty members. Faculty committees should be empowered to act upon the information gathered and to make recommendations for improvement.

Yale:

Departments and schools should regularly collect systematic written student evaluations of their courses and teachers.

9. CAMPUSWIDE COUNCILS AND SENATES

A. Existing Campuswide Councils and Senates[1]

Columbia University: University Senate

Powers: A policy-making body that may consider all matters of universitywide concern or matters affecting more than one faculty or school. Acts of the senate are final unless concurrence of the trustees is required. The executive committee of the senate is empowered to work with the board of trustees in the selection of six mutually agreed upon trustees and is also to be consulted on the appointment of senior universitywide officers and senior academic officials, including the president and provost. "The several schools, faculties, and departments will continue to exercise their present functions and powers respecting appointment, curriculum, educational standards and policy, internal decision-making, and such administrative matters as pertain solely to an individual school, faculty or department. The Senate is authorized to act only in respect of questions involving more than one faculty or administrative board."

Composition: 100 members: 45 tenured faculty, 14 nontenured faculty (both full- and part-time), 20 students, 7 administrators (including the president and provost), 6 representatives of affiliated institutions, 2 library staff, 2 research staff, 2 administrative staff, 2 alumni. The president of the university is the presiding officer of the senate.

Election of members: Tenured and nontenured faculty representatives are elected separately, each directly from constituencies of school or faculty. Student representatives are elected either directly by students of a school or faculty or indirectly by the divisional student government. Administrators include the president and academic vice-president as ex officio members and five other administrators appointed by the president. Membership is for two-year terms. "No representative shall be elected from any group in the University unless at least 40 percent of the designated electorate has voted in the election in which he was chosen."

[1] For detailed case studies of four campuswide senates, see David Dill, *Case Studies in University Governance*, National Association of State Universities and Land-Grant Colleges, Washington, D.C., 1971.

Special features: Committees on Educational Policy and Development; Budget Review; Physical Development of the University; Faculty Affairs, Academic Freedom and Tenure (a committee of faculty only); Student Affairs (a committee of students only); External Relations and Research Policy; Community Relations; Rules of University Conduct; Alumni Relations; Honors and Prizes; Libraries; Senate Structure and Operations. The chief committee is the Executive Committee which sets the agenda of the senate and serves as committee on committees. Committees are responsible to the senate and report out recommendations for action by the senate as a whole. Membership on most committees is not limited to senators. "Faculty and student service on the Executive Committee will be time consuming. To the extent possible, teachers serving on it should be allowed a reduction in their teaching loads. Faculties and departments should also be requested to grant appropriate point credit to students for their participation."

Ohio State University: University Senate[2]

Powers: The senate is the principal legislative body of the multicampus university. Subject to the authority of the Board of Trustees, the senate has the following powers:

1 "Under delegation by the University Faculty—to establish the educational and academic policies of the University; to recommend the establishment, abolition, and alteration of educational units and programs of study; to recommend to the Board of Trustees candidates for Honorary Degrees; to recommend candidates for degrees and certificates (which power shall be reserved to the faculty and administrative members of the University Senate).

2 "To consider, to make recommendations concerning, and (in pursuance of rules pertaining to the University) to act upon matters relating to the rights, responsibilities, and concerns of students, faculty, administrators, and staff."

The senators representing the administration, the faculty, or the students may meet separately or organize themselves as they choose; however the Senate is independent of each of these bodies and can act without their concurrence or review.

Composition: 132 voting members: 24 administration members

[2] The University Senate has been in existence since September 1972.

ex officio, 68 faculty members and 40 student members. The president of the university is the presiding officer of the senate.

Election of members: The 24 administration members serve ex officio and have no fixed terms. The faculty representatives are elected by faculty members on regular contract from election districts of each college, the regional campus, the library, and the combined Departments of Military, Naval and Air Force Aerospace Studies. Faculty members serve three-year staggered terms, and are ineligible for reelection for one year. The student members include the president of the Undergraduate Student Government, ex officio; 6 representatives from residential and individual campus student associations; 15 from individual colleges and regional campuses; and one each to represent black students, the Women's Self-Government Association, and the fraternity council; 5 graduate representatives of professional schools; and 10 graduate students, one from each graduate area. Student representatives must be in good standing and enrolled each quarter. They serve for one-year terms and are eligible for reelection.

Special features: Action by the senate is by a majority of members present and voting. The senate meets monthly, and meetings are open to the public and the media unless they have been ruled closed by the program committee. "Student members shall not be penalized for missing classes and related academic activities while attending meetings of the Senate or its committees. Students will be expected to complete usual course requirements."

Committees: There are three organizing committees, restricted in membership to members of the senate. Other committees are not limited to members of the senate. The Steering Committee is the senate's committee on committees. "Its elected members shall be an advisory group available to both the President and the Board of Trustees for advice and counsel on any matter relating to the operation and development of the University." The chairman of the Steering Committee is elected from among the faculty members of the Committee. The Program Committee receives proposals for senate action and sets the agenda; it also serves as liaison between the senate and the three campus constituencies and the university at large. The Committee on Rules and Senate Organization has "continuing responsibility for assessing the structure, operation, and effectiveness of the Senate. . . ."

Princeton University: The Council of the Princeton University Community

Powers: An advisory body to consider and investigate any policy or general issue related to the university and to make recommendations to decision-making bodies or officers. To make rules of conduct or to delegate authority to make them and to oversee their application are direct responsibilities of the council. Special responsibilities continue to reside in the Faculty Assembly and the Undergraduate Assembly on questions which are directly relevant to their members. The council does not deal with questions of appointment and advancement of individual faculty members, and the faculty continues to bear major responsibility for academic policy.

Composition: 57 members: 7 senior administrative officers including the president and provost, 18 faculty, 14 undergraduates, 8 graduate students, 4 alumni, 5 staff, 1 from other groups. The president of the university is the presiding officer of the council and chairman of the executive committee.

Election of members:[3] Faculty members are elected at large according to the single transferable vote system, modified to ensure representation of nontenured faculty. They serve three-year staggered terms. Undergraduate representatives are elected by the Undergraduate Assembly, according to the single transferable vote system, modified to ensure that at least four undergraduates who are not in the assembly are elected to the council. Undergraduates serve one-year terms. The graduate student representatives are elected by a universitywide body representing graduate students, according to the single transferable vote system, modified to ensure representation from each division. They serve two-year staggered terms. Representatives from staff and professional library staff are elected respectively by the Staff Council and a meeting of the professional library staff, according to the system of the alternative vote. They serve two-year staggered terms. The alumni representatives are elected by the Alumni Council and serve two-year staggered terms.

[3] See Voting Procedures below.

Special features: Committees: Executive; Rights and Rules; Governance; Priorities (committee concerned with the budget, of which the Provost is chairman); Relations with the Local Community; Resources; Judicial. The Executive Committee is composed of 15 members of the council, with the president of the university as chairman; members are chosen from among those on the council by their constituents. Members of the six other committees may be persons not on the council.

Voting procedures: An explanation of the alternate vote:

"The alternate vote is characteristically used in elections in which more than two candidates compete for a single position. A simple majority of the votes cast is needed for election.

"Let us hypothesize an election in which four candidates compete for one position, and 100 voters cast ballots. . . . The first choices of the voters are tabulated (see Table 1, column A). Since no candidate has received a majority of the votes cast, the candidate with the fewest votes (Baker) is eliminated. Each ballot indicating him as first choice is now awarded to the candidates listed on the ballot as the second choice. The redistribution of Baker's seven ballots is shown in column B. New totals for the remaining candidates are tabulated (see column C). Since no candidate has yet achieved a majority, the candidate with the fewest votes (Carter) is eliminated; each of his ballots is redistributed to the remaining candidate indicated as the next best alternative. This redistribution is shown in column D. New totals for Ames and Daniels are tabulated. Ames now has 49 votes, and Daniels has 51. Daniels is elected."

TABLE 1	A	B	C	D	E
Ames	41	1	42	7	49
Baker	7				
Carter	16	6	22		
Daniels	36	0	36	15	51

An explanation of the single transferable vote:

"The single transferable vote is characteristically used in elections in which many candidates compete for several positions. Let us hypothesize an election in which five candidates are running for two positions and ballots are cast by 150 voters.

"The number of votes needed for election (the quota) is given by the formula

$$\frac{\text{number of votes cast}}{\text{number of positions to be filled} + 1} + 1$$

In our example, the quota is 51.

"In casting ballots, the voters are instructed to rank the candidates in order of preference. The first choices of the voters are then tabulated, and any candidate receiving the quota is elected. If his total exceeds the quota, the extra votes are redistributed among the remaining candidates. Column A, Table 2, lists the number of first-choice votes cast for each of the five candidates in our example. Since Alcott has 76 first-choice votes, 25 votes must be redistributed. There are two alternative methods of redistribution:

1 Each of the remaining candidates is awarded a percentage of the number of ballots to be redistributed equal to the percentage of second-choice votes he received on all ballots on which the elected candidate was the first choice. This is the method that makes complete use of the information voters have provided about their preferences, and by computer, such calculations can be made quickly.

2 The proper number of ballots (in this case, 25) is drawn at random from among all the ballots cast for the elected man (Alcott). Each of these ballots is awarded to the candidate indicated as the second choice (see column B, Table 2). A new tabulation of votes is made (see column C). Since none of the four candidates has passed the quota, the candidate with the fewest votes (Clark) is eliminated. Each of his ballots is awarded to the remaining candidate indicated as the next best alternative. The results of this redistribution are shown in column D. Column E shows the new totals for the remaining candidates. The redistribution of Clark's votes has not caused any of the three remaining candidates to pass the quota. Therefore, the candidate with the fewest votes (Eaton) is eliminated, and his votes are redistributed as shown in column F. A new tabulation of the total vote is given in column G. Baker, with 52 votes, is elected. Both positions are now filled, and the election is completed.

"Let us suppose that the election rules stipulate that at least one of the two positions must be filled by an undergraduate and that, of the five original candidates, only two, Clark and Eaton, are undergraduates. After Alcott's extra votes were redistributed, Clark had the fewest votes and was, therefore, eliminated. If at least one undergraduate must be elected, Eaton cannot be eliminated. He is therefore elected, both positions have been filled; and, in accordance with the rules, at least one undergraduate has been elected."

TABLE 2

	A	B	C	D	E	F	G
Alcott	76						
Baker	18	8	26	15	41	11	52
*Clark**	17	6	22				
Dent	21	4	26	5	31	16	47
*Eaton**	18	7	25	2	27		

* Undergraduates

University of Minnesota: University Senate[4] The University Senate is a multicampus structure. With the exception of grading policy, which is a campus matter, most university business is treated as all-university business and therefore comes before the senate. Each campus also has a Campus Assembly responsible for educational matters concerning that campus; members of the University Senate from each campus are among the members of the Campus Assembly.

The faculty representatives to the University Senate comprise the Faculty Senate, and the elected student representatives comprise the Student Senate.

Powers: "The University Senate has general legislative authority over educational matters concerning more than one campus or the University as a whole but not over the internal affairs of a single campus, institute, college, or school . . . ." This includes authority over minimal requirements for a liberal education, power to enact regulations for governing of faculty and students with respect to their relations with the university as a whole, power to recognize campus legislative and policy-making bodies as official, and power to delegate authority and responsibility to single campus assemblies in educational matters concerning that one campus.

[4] The University Senate has been in existence since October 1912, but was reorganized in July 1969. Students have been on senate committees since the 1940s. They were made officially part of the body in 1969, however.

The University Senate may delegate specific functions to the Faculty Senate or the Student Senate exclusively. Generally, the functions of the Student Senate include student government, student organizations and publications. Functions of the Faculty Senate include "accreditation, designation and granting of University honors, policies concerning faculty appointment and tenure, and matters within the jurisdiction of the Faculty Affairs and Judicial Committees."

Composition: President of the university, who is chairman of the senate; 48 members of the all-university Administrative Committee as nonvoting, ex officio members; 17 members of the Senate Consultative Committee as ex officio voting members (10 faculty and 7 students); 136 elected representatives of the faculty; and 63 elected representatives of the students.

Election of members: Faculty representatives are elected from among regular, full-time faculty by secret ballot by the several institutes, colleges, or schools. They serve three-year terms and are eligible for reelection only after a one-year interval. Student representatives are elected from among undergraduate, graduate, and general extension students by secret ballot by the several institutes, colleges or schools. They serve one-year terms and are eligible for reelection for up to three consecutive terms.

Special features: Most of the senate's work is done in committee. The Senate Consultative Committee serves as a consultative body to the president and as the Executive Committee of the senate; it has power to recommend that particular functions be acted upon exclusively by either the Faculty Senate or the Student Senate. It meets regularly with the president. Its members are elected at large. Other standing committees of the senate include Committee on Senate Committees, Academic Standing and Relations, Administrative, Educational Policy, Faculty Affairs (faculty only), Judicial (faculty only), Library, Research, Resources and Planning.

University of New Hampshire: University Senate [5]

Powers: The only legislative body for universitywide policy, subject always to approval by the board of trustees. A unicameral senate with supporting faculty and student caucuses which are comprised of members of the senate. The student under-

[5] The University Senate has been in existence since May 1969.

graduate caucus replaces the student senate, and organizations supported by the student activity tax are under its jurisdiction. The university senate has jurisdiction in all matters of student government, faculty government, and educational policy; it can delegate specific jurisdictions to the faculty or the student caucuses at its discretion.

Composition: 77 voting members: 30 faculty, 12 administrators, 30 students, and 5 graduate students. Chairman of the senate is to be elected by its members. Three caucuses are structures supportive of the senate. One is comprised of faculty senators; one of undergraduate student senators; and the third of graduate student senators. By a two-thirds vote a caucus may decide that an item requires action by an exceptional majority of two-thirds of the senate. Originally, a provision was made for three forums; one of all faculty members, one of all undergraduate students, and the third of all graduate students. The forums would meet monthly to advise their respective caucuses. These forums have been eliminated.

Election of senate members: All senators are elected from single member districts of approximately equal size. Faculty are elected on the basis of department and college; full-time faculty only. They serve three-year staggered terms, without consecutive election. Undergraduate students are elected from districts constructed on the basis of residence for those living on campus and from commuters' districts constructed on the basis of college; full-time undergraduates only. They serve one-year terms and are eligible for reelection. Graduate students are from districts drawn on the same basis as faculty; full-time graduate students only.

Special features: Executive Council organizes the work of the Senate. The president of the university is its chairman, and it includes among its members the academic vice-president, chairmen of the Faculty Caucus, the Student Caucus, and the Graduate Student Caucus. It functions as advisory to the President of the university, assigns work to senate committees, prepares the agenda for senate meetings and acts on an interim basis between senate meetings.

Committees: In addition to old standing committees: University Planning, Financial Aids, Student Welfare, Faculty Welfare. "With respect to Administrative and joint Faculty-Administrative committees, student membership would be determined by the Executive Council of the University Senate."

University of Toronto: The Governing Council The principles recommended in 1970 by the Commission on the Government of the University of Toronto were adopted in the University of Toronto Act, 1971. A single Governing Council has been established for the university, with the powers and duties of both the governing board and the senate.[6]

Powers: "The government, management and control of the University . . . and of the property, revenues, business and affairs thereof, and the powers and duties of the governors of the University of Toronto and of the Senate of the University . . . are vested in the Governing Council . . . ." Included in the Council's powers are appointment of the President; appointment, promotion, and removal of teaching and administrative staffs and other employees; establishment of new faculties; admission standards; delegation of its powers; as well as handling of property, investments, and borrowing of money. The Governors of the University are continued as a corporation under the name Governing Council of the University of Toronto.

Composition:[7]   50 members: chancellor and president as ex officio members; 2 officers of the university and its federated colleges and universities, appointed by the president; 16 members, none of whom are students, administrators, or teaching staff, appointed by the Lieutenant Governor in council; 12 teaching staff members, elected by the teaching staff; 8 student members, 4 of whom are elected by and from undergraduate students, 2 of whom are elected by and from graduate students, and 2 of whom are elected by and from part-time students; 2 administrative staff elected by administrative staff; 8 alumni who are not students, nor teaching staff, nor administrative staff, elected by alumni. Student members and members appointed by the president have one-year terms. After the ini-

[6] The new Governing Council has been in operation since July 1, 1972.

[7] The composition of the council varies somewhat from the recommendations of the University Commission on Government that are quoted in other sections of this Appendix.

tial elections, all other members serve for three-year staggered terms.

Special features: After initial appointments, the chairman and the vice-chairman of the Governing Council to be elected by the council from among all the members appointed by the Lieutenant Governor in Council. An Executive Committee of 14 members of the council, including chairman of the council and president as ex officio; the other 12 members to be appointed annually by constituency within the council. The chairman of the Governing Council is chairman of the Executive Committee. "The Executive Committee may deal with any matter that is within the responsibility of the Governing Council, but no decision of the Executive Committee is effective until approved by the Governing Council or unless the Governing Council has previously assigned authority therefore to the Executive Committee."

B. Proposals for Campuswide Councils

Harvard University The Governance Committee at Harvard tentatively recommended in 1972 (in *Tentative Recommendations Concerning a University Senate and Council of Deans*) that:

1 A University-wide Senate should be established as a deliberative and advisory, but not legislative, form. The Senate would be granted authority to:

(a) Consider any question which concerns more than one Faculty or which is of University-wide significance.

(b) Receive, discuss and disseminate information concerning any such question.

(c) Conduct studies, make recommendations and enact resolutions concerning any such question.

(d) Request information through appropriate channels from any component of the University.

2 The Senate would be composed of faculty members and students elected from the various schools . . . .

All questions concerning the mode of election and qualifications (e.g., subject matter of departmental representation, tenure or non-tenure status, etc.) would be decided by the individual Faculties.

Deans of Faculties, the President's principal administrative officers, three representatives of the Associated Harvard Alumni, and one representative of the Radcliffe Alumnae Association would have the privileges of the floor but would not be voting members.

3 Nothing should preclude either the faculty or student members of the Senate from meeting separately if it seems appropriate for them to do so.

4 The President of the University or his designee would be the presiding officer of the Senate.

5 The Senate would have a steering committee consisting of eight faculty members and four students elected by and from those eligible to serve in each case [from among the various schools]. . . .

The President of the University or his designee would be chairman of the steering committee. The vice chairman of the steering committee would be a faculty member elected by the members of the steering committee.

The steering committee would be the most important committee of the Senate. It would, among other things, schedule the Senate's meetings, determine the Senate's agenda, recommend establishment and the duties of other committees, serve as the primary liaison with the President and other components of the University, and, pursuant to the general policies established by the Senate, administer the affairs of the Senate when the Senate was not in session. As in the case of the Senate members, nothing should preclude the faculty and student members of the steering committee from meeting separately if it seems appropriate for them to do so.

6 The Senate would function primarily through committees. The committees would be established, and their responsibilities determined, by the Senate. Members of committees would be appointed by the President in consultation with the vice chairman of the steering committee. Members of committees could be selected from the entire University community.

7 A central feature of the Senate is that it would develop in an evolutionary manner. Thus in its initial stages the Senate, in collaboration with the President, would make tentative decisions concerning its priorities, its relationships with other components of the University and its general mode of operation. Rigid jurisdictional lines would not be drawn. Flexibility, cooperation and experimentation would be emphasized.

8 "The structure and activities of the Senate should be systematically examined four years after the Senate is established."

Yale University The Yale Study Commission on Governance rejected the idea of a campuswide representative assembly, and recommended instead campuswide advisory councils, with several stand-by forums to enhance public discussion. An all-university representative assembly was rejected because "an assembly of even as many as two hundred members, which is as large as hopes for sustained discussion permit, is so small, relative to the number of faculty, students, and staff it is designed to represent, that its members would be at a loss to know the opinions of constituents and would themselves be dependent, for obtaining that information, on some such system of forums as here proposed. An assembly would be neither as expert as the advisory councils can be nor as conducive to genuine participation and representation of views as forums permit. For University governance, it falls between two stools."

The Study Commission proposed four types of structures for governing the university as a whole:

1 All-university advisory councils to be established by the president and to be composed of faculty, students, nonfaculty employees, alumni, and administrators. There would be about 14 members on each council, which would be advisory to the trustees and the administrative officers. There would be one such council in each of the following areas: priorities and planning, institutional policies, investments and finance, operations and services.

2 Stand-by forums to provide wider opportunities for participation by more than just the members of the advisory councils. Forums would regularize and enhance direct participation in policy debate.

Faculty: each faculty would expand its considerations to general university policy and would have an advisory role with respect to such policy, as distinguished from its authority over internal academic policies.

Nonfaculty and student forums: each undergraduate college, professional school, division with the graduate school, and each category of nonfaculty employees would have a steering committee to convene and conduct open meetings for all members of that group.

3 Policy Review Commission—a structure to enhance the accountability of the president, other administrative officers, and trustees by providing specific occasions for requesting justification of policy and further information. The commission would have 35 members including faculty, students, non-faculty employees, and alumni.

4 Committees on University Services—committees to include those per-

sons who make use of the service as well as those who manage and staff it; to advise on policies and operations. One such committee on each of the following: libraries, health services, museums, computing operations.

C. Other Recommendations Concerning Councils

ACE "As an aid to effective decision-making, joint administrative-faculty-student committees should be established, wherever possible, to assist in resolving the problem and attaining the objective. More institutions should experiment with permanent legislative assemblies composed of administrators, faculty, and students. Some issues are better dealt with by faculty assemblies, some by student groups, and some by the president and his administrative staff; but each group's decision-making processes can benefit from inputs from the other groups. There are, additionally, issues of concern to all three groups which should be dealt with by a governance system in which all are recognized as legitimate participants."

American Academy of Arts and Sciences, Assembly on University Goals and Governance "The tendency to create unicameral legislative or advisory bodies for colleges and universities raises the possibility that important issues specific to either faculty or students will be obfuscated. Where such councils or campus-wide senates are established, separate faculty, student and other deliberative bodies should also be maintained."

10.   OPENNESS OF DECISION MAKING AND COMMUNICATIONS

Toronto:

That openness, defined as follows, be accepted as a basic operating principle for all university councils and committees:

- that meetings of all university councils and committees be open to members of the university community, university media, the mass media, and members of the general community;

- that these meetings may move into camera by the vote of a simple majority of the members present, the reasons for doing so to be made explicit before a vote can be taken. [Editorial note: While the basic principle of openness is valid, not all committees comply with it: for example, the Executive Committee of the Governing Council and the Honorary Degrees Committee meet in closed session.]

American Academy of Arts and Sciences, Assembly on University Goals and Governance

If the internal and external constituencies of a college or university are to be kept properly informed, effective use of the written word is required. The many publications issued by departments, faculties and schools, including college catalogues, faculty handbooks, student guides, financial aid bulletins, weekly calendars, alumni magazines and fund-raising literature, together represent a considerable financial investment. Their purpose—to expound the institution's activities and goals—is insufficiently achieved. As a result, those who are not actually in the institution (and many who are) have only the most rudimentary notion of what in fact is happening. All such publications should more deliberately seek to reflect the institution's character and specific programs.

Colleges and universities ought to have a "Hansard" or regular publication reporting on all specific actions, executive, adjudicative and legislative, taken by trustee, faculty, student, staff and administrative groups. Similarly, such a publication should make available information about major contemplated policies or decisions on the part of any or all of the above groups. When possible, there should be sufficient time for comments and criticisms to be prepared and included in this publication.

Princeton:

That more information and more accurate information regarding the organization of the University and of its procedures for setting policy be regularly published in *The Undergraduate Announcement, The Graduate Announcement,* and the *General Catalogue.*

That the organization of the University and its procedures for setting policy regularly be made a subject for discussion with freshmen, new graduate students, and new members of the faculty and staff.

That the Administration encourage the hiring of student administrative assistants by both the academic and non-academic departments of the University.

That the Secretary of the University develop procedures for making documents relating to the governing of the University and to current issues of University policy easily available to members of the University community at Firestone Library and at the various branch libraries.

The President of the University, annually and early in the fall term, report on the state of the University, and suggest the problems and goals of most immediacy to it, in a public and joint meeting of the Council of the Princeton University Community, the Faculty, the Undergraduate Assembly, and the Staff Council.

That the University publish its *Newsletter* more frequently, consider revisions in its composition, and distribute it to students as well as to members of the faculty and staff.

That the *Daily Princetonian* consider ways to broaden its readership in the University community and its coverage of the discussions in, and the decisions of, decision-making bodies.

ACE:

How to keep the channels open will present a different problem on every campus. Nevertheless, it should always be possible for a student, faculty member, trustee, or layman who has a message to get through to the president. Accessibility, moreover, is not the whole answer. Presidents and other administrators must take positive steps to explain their plans and policies to the appropriate constituencies, through such devices as newsletters, annual reports, "town meetings," or position papers on particular issues. They must also provide students, faculty, and others with information sufficiently in advance to enable them to make meaningful contributions to decisions.

To communicate effectively administrators must be open and candid in giving reasons for decisions and actions. There are instances when the release of information would needlessly injure individuals. But the withholding of information on such occasions will be better understood and accepted if, at all other times, communication is candid. Here, also, continuing efforts are as important as those during crisis. Administrators should meet frequently with faculty and student groups, not only to listen but also to make known their thinking on basic issues.

The ability of presidents and other administrative officers to devote the time required for the communications we consider desirable is dependent on adequate institutional staffing.

Every attempt must be made to establish effective communications, so that policy questions and grievances can be aired by the campus community. A number of institutions have had success with such communications methods as (1) centralized files of important institutional records accessible to campus constituents; (2) rumor centers, especially during periods of campus turmoil, to which members of the community may telephone for accurate and up-to-date information; (3) ombudsmen to hear grievances, speed up communications, and unsnarl red tape; and (4) "official" campus newspapers, in which texts of important reports and other documents of wide interest to the campus community can appear. Members of the campus community should recognize, however, that improved channels of consultation may render decision-making procedures slower and more cumbersome.

Yale:

As a matter of principle, because of the unique nature of an academic community, general information pertinent to policy making should always be ultimately accessible to its members. When such information is not immediately accessible it should be regarded as "postponed", not "denied", and never "concealed". The burden of proof must be placed on the information-possessing agency as to why general information relevant to policy making should be withheld; the seeker of such information should not have to justify his need for it.

Believing that improvement in communications is its highest priority, the Yale Commission also proposes the following specific reforms:

- A "Public Affairs" Information Office—The President and Corporation should establish and maintain with wholly adequate financial support a 'public affairs' information office in which written and oral information is made easily available to students, as well as to faculty and staff. . . . it should organize each fall a set of open meetings with presentations followed by questions from the floor in which Yale's governance is explained and special attention is given to channels through which members of the Yale community can influence policy.

- A News Bulletin—For the same reasons, the administration should publish weekly, monthly, or irregularly as special needs arise a news bulletin or greatly extended University Calendar. The new publication should announce policy decisions reached by various officers and bodies within the University. It should also be employed, as needed, to explain policies.

- Financing the Office of Institutional Research—The President and Provost should provide sufficient funds and authorization to the Office of Institutional Research to permit it to become a general resource in University decision making.

- Reports on Faculty Meetings—After each school faculty meeting, a dean or other responsible spokesman for the faculty should, without undue delay, be available at an announced time and place to report on the faculty meeting to interested students and representatives from student publications.

- Reports on Corporation Meetings—Within a day or so after each Corporation meeting, the President should be available at an announced time and place to report on and answer questions about the meeting, for the benefit of representatives of student publications and other interested students, faculty, and staff.

- A Policy Review Commission of 35 members (faculty, students, and nonfaculty employees) to conduct a regularized interview of University administrative officers in which officers are asked to explain their decisions and policies.

Appendix D: Statements by the American Association of University Professors

1940 Statement of Principles on Academic Freedom and Tenure

Statement on Government of Colleges and Universities (1966)

Student Participation in College and University Government: A Report of Committee T (1970)

Faculty Participation in the Selection and Retention of Administrators: A Report by Committee T (1972)

Statement on Collective Bargaining (1972)

Statement on Procedural Standards in the Renewal or Nonrenewal of Faculty Appointments (1971)

The purpose of this statement is to promote public understanding and support of academic freedom and tenure and agreement upon procedures to assure them in colleges and universities. Institutions of higher education are conducted for the common good and not to further the interest of either the individual teacher[1] or the institution as a whole. The common good depends upon the free search for truth and its free exposition.

Academic freedom is essential to these purposes and applies to both teaching and research. Freedom in research is fundamental to the advancement of truth. Academic freedom in its teaching aspect is fundamental for the protection of the rights of the teacher in teaching and of the student to freedom in learning. It carries with it duties correlative with rights.

Tenure is a means to certain ends; specifically: (1) Freedom of teaching and research and of extramural activities and (2) a sufficient degree of economic security to make the profession attractive to men and women of ability. Freedom and economic security, hence, tenure, are indispensable to the success of an institution in fulfilling its obligations to its students and to society.

Academic freedom

1 The teacher is entitled to full freedom in research and in the publication of the results, subject to the adequate performance of his other academic duties; but research for pecuniary return should be based upon an understanding with the authorities of the institution.

2 The teacher is entitled to freedom in the classroom in discussing his subject, but he should be careful not to introduce into his teaching controversial matter which has no relation to his subject. Limitations of academic freedom because of religious or other aims of the institution should be clearly stated in writing at the time of the appointment.

---

[1] The word "teacher" as used in this document is understood to include the investigator who is attached to an academic institution without teaching duties.

SOURCE: Reprinted from *AAUP Policy Documents and Reports*, 1971 Edition.

3 The college or university teacher is a citizen, a member of a learned profession, and an officer of an educational institution. When he speaks or writes as a citizen, he should be free from institutional censorship or discipline, but his special position in the community imposes special obligations. As a man of learning and an educational officer, he should remember that the public may judge his profession and his institution by his utterances. Hence he should at all times be accurate, should exercise appropriate restraint, should show respect for the opinions of others, and should make every effort to indicate that he is not an institutional spokesman.

Academic tenure

After the expiration of a probationary period, teachers or investigators should have permanent or continuous tenure, and their service should be terminated only for adequate cause, except in the case of retirement for age, or under extraordinary circumstances because of financial exigencies.

In the interpretation of this principle it is understood that the following represents acceptable academic practice:

1 The precise terms and conditions of every appointment should be stated in writing and be in the possession of both institution and teacher before the appointment is consummated.

2 Beginning with appointment to the rank of full-time instructor or a higher rank, the probationary period should not exceed seven years, including within this period full-time service in all institutions of higher education; but subject to the proviso that when, after a term of probationary service of more than three years in one or more institutions, a teacher is called to another institution it may be agreed in writing that his new appointment is for a probationary period of not more than four years, even though thereby the person's total probationary period in the academic profession is extended beyond the normal maximum of seven years. Notice should be given at least one year prior to the expiration of the probationary period if the teacher is not to be continued in service after the expiration of that period.

3 During the probationary period a teacher should have the academic freedom that all other members of the faculty have.

4 Termination for cause of a continuous appointment, or the dismissal for cause of a teacher previous to the expiration of a term appointment, should, if possible, be considered by both a faculty committee and the governing board of the institution. In all cases where the facts are in dispute, the accused teacher should be informed before the hearing in writing of the charges against him and should have the opportunity to be heard in his own defense by all bodies that pass judgment upon his case. He should be permitted to have with him an adviser of his own choosing who may act as counsel. There should be a full stenographic record of the hearing available to the parties concerned. In the hearing of charges of incompetence the testimony should include that of teachers and other scholars, either from his own or from other institutions. Teachers on continuous appointment who are dismissed for reasons not involving moral turpitude should receive their salaries for at least a year from the date of notification of dismissal whether or not they are continued in their duties at the institution.

5 Termination of a continuous appointment because of financial exigency should be demonstrably bona fide.

Statement on Government of Colleges and Universities, 1966

INTRODUCTION This Statement is a call to mutual understanding regarding the government of colleges and universities. Understanding, based on community of interest, and producing joint effort, is essential for at least three reasons. First, the academic institution, public or private, often has become less autonomous; buildings, research, and student tuition are supported by funds over which the college or university exercises a diminishing control. Legislative and executive governmental authority, at all levels, plays a part in the making of important decisions in academic policy. If these voices and forces are to be successfully heard and integrated, the academic institution must be in a position to meet them with its own generally unified view. Second, regard for the welfare of the institution remains important despite the mobility and interchange of scholars. Third, a college or university in which all the components are aware of their interdependence, of the usefulness of communication among themselves, and of the force of joint action will enjoy increased capacity to solve educational problems.

THE ACADEMIC INSTITUTION: JOINT EFFORT *Preliminary considerations* The variety and complexity of the tasks performed by institutions of higher education produce an inescapable interdependence among governing board, administration, faculty, students, and others. The relationship calls for adequate communication among these components, and full opportunity for appropriate joint planning and effort.

Joint effort in an academic institution will take a variety of forms appropriate to the kinds of situations encountered. In some instances, an initial exploration or recommendation will be made by the president with consideration by the faculty at a later stage; in other instances, a first and essentially definitive recommendation will be made by the faculty, subject to the endorsement of the president and the governing board. In still others, a substantive contribution can be made when student leaders are responsibly involved in the process. Although the variety of such approaches may be wide, at least two general conclusions regarding joint effort seem clearly warranted: (1)

SOURCE: Reprinted from *AAUP Policy Documents and Reports*, 1973 Edition.

important areas of action involve at one time or another the initiating capacity and decision-making participation of all the institutional components, and (2) differences in the weight of each voice, from one point to the next, should be determined by reference to the responsibility of each component for the particular matter at hand, as developed hereinafter.

Determination of general educational policy   The general educational policy, i.e., the objectives of an institution and the nature, range, and pace of its efforts, is shaped by the institutional charter or by law, by tradition and historical development, by the present needs of the community of the institution, and by the professional aspirations and standards of those directly involved in its work. Every board will wish to go beyond its formal trustee obligation to conserve the accomplishment of the past and to engage seriously with the future; every faculty will seek to conduct an operation worthy of scholarly standards of learning; every administrative officer will strive to meet his charge and to attain the goals of the institution. The interests of all are coordinate and related, and unilateral effort can lead to confusion or conflict. Essential to a solution is a reasonably explicit statement on general educational policy. Operating responsibility and authority, and procedures for continuing review, should be clearly defined in official regulations.

When an educational goal has been established, it becomes the responsibility primarily of the faculty to determine appropriate curriculum and procedures of student instruction.

Special considerations may require particular accommodations: (1) a publicly supported institution may be regulated by statutory provisions, and (2) a church-controlled institution may be limited by its charter or bylaws. When such external requirements influence course content and manner of instruction or research, they impair the educational effectiveness of the institution.

Such matters as major changes in the size or composition of the student body and the relative emphasis to be given to the various elements of the educational and research program should involve participation of governing board, administration, and faculty prior to final decision.

Internal operations of the institution   The framing and execution of long-range plans, one of the most important aspects of institutional responsibility, should be a central and continuing concern in the academic community.

Effective planning demands that the broadest possible exchange of information and opinion should be the rule for communication among the components of a college or university. The channels of communication should be established and maintained by joint endeavor. Distinction should be observed between the institutional system of communication and the system of responsibility for the making of decisions.

A second area calling for joint effort in internal operations is that of decisions regarding existing or prospective physical resources. The board, president, and faculty should all seek agreement on basic decisions regarding buildings and other facilities to be used in the educational work of the institution.

A third area is budgeting. The allocation of resources among competing demands is central in the formal responsibility of the governing board, in the administrative authority of the president, and in the educational function of the faculty. Each component should therefore have a voice in the determination of short- and long-range priorities, and each should receive appropriate analyses of past budgetary experience, reports on current budgets and expenditures, and short- and long-range budgetary projections. The function of each component in budgetary matters should be understood by all; the allocation of authority will determine the flow of information and the scope of participation in decisions.

Joint effort of a most critical kind must be taken when an institution chooses a new president. The selection of a chief administrative officer should follow upon cooperative search by the governing board and the faculty, taking into consideration the opinions of others who are appropriately interested. The president should be equally qualified to serve both as the executive officer of the governing board and as the chief academic officer of the institution and the faculty. His dual role requires that he be able to interpret to board and faculty the educational views and concepts of institutional government of the other. He should have the confidence of the board and the faculty.

The selection of academic deans and other chief academic officers should be the responsibility of the president with the advice of and in consultation with the appropriate faculty.

Determinations of faculty status, normally based on the recommendations of the faculty groups involved, are discussed in
Part V of this Statement; but it should here be noted that the
building of a strong faculty requires careful joint effort in such
actions as staff selection and promotion and the granting of
tenure. Joint action should also govern dismissals; the applica-
ble principles and procedures in these matters are well established.[1]

External relations of the institution Anyone—a member of the
governing board, the president or other member of the administration, a member of the faculty, or a member of the
student body or the alumni—affects the institution when he
speaks of it in public. An individual who speaks unofficially
should so indicate. An official spokesman for the institution,
the board, the administration, the faculty, or the student body
should be guided by established policy.

It should be noted that only the board speaks legally for the
whole institution, although it may delegate responsibility to an
agent.

The right of a board member, an administrative officer, a faculty member, or a student to speak on general educational questions or about the administration and operations of his own institution is a part of his right as a citizen and should not be
abridged by the institution.[2] There exist, of course, legal
bounds relating to defamation of character, and there are questions of propriety.

---

[1] See the 1940 *Statement of Principles on Academic Freedom and Tenure* and the
1958 *Statement on Procedural Standards in Faculty Dismissal Proceedings.* These
statements have been jointly approved or adopted by the Association of American Colleges and the American Association of University Professors; the 1940
Statement has been endorsed by numerous learned and scientific societies and
educational associations.

[2] With respect to faculty members, the 1940 *Statement of Principles on Academic
Freedom and Tenure* reads: "The college or university teacher is a citizen, a
member of a learned profession, and an officer of an educational institution.
When he speaks or writes as a citizen, he should be free from institutional censorship or discipline, but his special position in the community imposes
special obligations. As a man of learning and an educational officer, he should
remember that the public may judge his profession and his institution by his
utterances. Hence he should at all times be accurate, should exercise appropriate restraint, should show respect for the opinion of others, and should make
every effort to indicate that he is not an institutional spokesman."

The governing board has a special obligation to assure that the history of the college or university shall serve as a prelude and inspiration to the future. The board helps relate the institution to its chief community: e.g., the community college to serve the educational needs of a defined population area or group, the church-controlled college to be cognizant of the announced position of its denomination, and the comprehensive university to discharge the many duties and to accept the appropriate new challenges which are its concern at the several levels of higher education.

The governing board of an institution of higher education in the United States operates, with few exceptions, as the final institutional authority. Private institutions are established by charters; public institutions are established by constitutional or statutory provisions. In private institutions the board is frequently self-perpetuating; in public colleges and universities the present membership of a board may be asked to suggest candidates for appointment. As a whole and individually when the governing board confronts the problem of succession, serious attention should be given to obtaining properly qualified persons. Where public law calls for election of governing board members, means should be found to insure the nomination of fully suited persons, and the electorate should be informed of the relevant criteria for board membership.

Since the membership of the board may embrace both individual and collective competence of recognized weight, its advice or help may be sought through established channels by other components of the academic community. The governing board of an institution of higher education, while maintaining a general overview, entrusts the conduct of administration to the administrative officers, the president and the deans, and the conduct of teaching and research to the faculty. The board should undertake appropriate self-limitation.

One of the governing board's important tasks is to insure the publication of codified statements that define the over-all policies and procedures of the institution under its jurisdiction.

The board plays a central role in relating the likely needs of the future to predictable resources; it has the responsibility for husbanding the endowment; it is responsible for obtaining needed capital and operating funds; and in the broadest sense of the term it should pay attention to personnel policy. In order to fulfill these duties, the board should be aided by, and may insist upon, the development of long-range planning by the administration and faculty.

When ignorance or ill-will threatens the institution or any part of it, the governing board must be available for support. In grave crises it will be expected to serve as a champion. Although the action to be taken by it will usually be on behalf of the president, the faculty, or the student body, the board should make clear that the protection it offers to an individual or a group is, in fact, a fundamental defense of the vested interests of society in the educational institution.[3]

THE ACADEMIC INSTITUTION: THE PRESIDENT The president, as the chief executive officer of an institution of higher education, is measured largely by his capacity for institutional leadership. He shares responsibility for the definition and attainment of goals, for administrative action, and for operating the communications system which links the components of the academic community. He represents his institution to its many publics. His leadership role is supported by delegated authority from the board and faculty.

As the chief planning officer of an institution, the president has a special obligation to innovate and initiate. The degree to which a president can envision new horizons for his institution, and can persuade others to see them and to work toward them, will often constitute the chief measure of his administration.

The president must at times, with or without support, infuse new life into a department; relatedly, he may at times be required, working within the concept of tenure, to solve problems of obsolescence. The president will necessarily utilize the judgments of the faculty, but in the interest of academic standards he may also seek outside evaluations by scholars of acknowledged competence.

[3] The American Association of University Professors, recognizing the growth of autonomous state-wide bodies superordinate to existing Boards of Trustees, regards the objectives and practices recommended in the 1966 *Statement* as constituting equally appropriate guidelines for such bodies. As newer, and more influential components of the academic community, they bear particular responsibility for protecting the autonomy of individual institutions under their jurisdiction and for implementing policies of shared responsibility as outlined in Section II when they displace functions of institutional governing boards. (Adopted by the AAUP Council in May 1972.)

It is the duty of the president to see to it that the standards and procedures in operational use within the college or university conform to the policy established by the governing board and to the standards of sound academic practice. It is also incumbent on the president to insure that faculty views, including dissenting views, are presented to the board in those areas and on those issues where responsibilities are shared. Similarly the faculty should be informed of the views of the board and the administration on like issues.

The president is largely responsible for the maintenance of existing institutional resources and the creation of new resources; he has ultimate managerial responsibility for a large area of nonacademic activities, he is responsible for public understanding, and by the nature of his office is the chief spokesman of his institution. In these and other areas his work is to plan, to organize, to direct, and to represent. The presidential function should receive the general support of board and faculty.

THE ACADEMIC INSTITUTION: THE FACULTY The faculty has primary responsibility for such fundamental areas as curriculum, subject matter and methods of instruction, research, faculty status, and those aspects of student life which relate to the educational process. On these matters the power of review or final decision lodged in the governing board or delegated by it to the president should be exercised adversely only in exceptional circumstances, and for reasons communicated to the faculty. It is desirable that the faculty should, following such communication, have opportunity for further consideration and further transmittal of its views to the president or board. Budgets, manpower limitations, the time element, and the policies of other groups, bodies and agencies having jurisdiction over the institution may set limits to realization of faculty advice.

The faculty sets the requirements for the degrees offered in course, determines when the requirements have been met, and authorizes the president and board to grant the degrees thus achieved.

Faculty status and related matters are primarily a faculty responsibility; this area includes appointments, reappointments, decisions not to reappoint, promotions, the granting of tenure, and dismissal. The primary responsibility of the faculty for such matters is based upon the fact that its judgment is central to general educational policy. Furthermore, scholars in a particular field or activity have the chief competence for judging the work of their colleagues; in such competence it is implicit that responsibility exists for both adverse and favorable judgments. Likewise there is the more general competence of experienced faculty personnel committees having a broader charge. Determinations in these matters should first be by faculty action through established procedures, reviewed by the chief academic officers with the concurrence of the board. The governing board and president should, on questions of faculty status, as in other matters where the faculty has primary responsibility, concur with the faculty judgment except in rare instances and for compelling reasons which should be stated in detail.

The faculty should actively participate in the determination of policies and procedures governing salary increases.

The chairman or head of a department, who serves as the chief representative of his department within an institution, should be selected either by departmental election or by appointment following consultation with members of the department and of related departments; appointments should normally be in conformity with department members' judgment. The chairman or department head should not have tenure in his office; his tenure as a faculty member is a matter of separate right. He should serve for a stated term but without prejudice to re-election or to reappointment by procedures which involve appropriate faculty consultation. Board, administration, and faculty should all bear in mind that the department chairman has a special obligation to build a department strong in scholarship and teaching capacity.

Agencies for faculty participation in the government of the college or university should be established at each level where faculty responsibility is present. An agency should exist for the presentation of the views of the whole faculty. The structure and procedures for faculty participation should be designed, approved, and established by joint action of the components of the institution. Faculty representatives should be selected by the faculty according to procedures determined by the faculty.

The agencies may consist of meetings of all faculty members of a department, school, college, division, or university system, or may take the form of faculty-elected executive committees in departments and schools and a faculty-elected senate or council for larger divisions or the institution as a whole.

Among the means of communication among the faculty, administration, and governing board now in use are: (1) circulation of memoranda and reports by board committees, the administration, and faculty committees, (2) joint *ad hoc* committees, (3) standing liaison committees, (4) membership of faculty members on administrative bodies, and (5) membership of faculty members on governing boards. Whatever the channels of communication, they should be clearly understood and observed.

On student status

When students in American colleges and universities desire to participate responsibly in the government of the institution they attend, their wish should be recognized as a claim to opportunity both for educational experience and for involvement in the affairs of their college or university. Ways should be found to permit significant student participation within the limits of attainable effectiveness. The obstacles to such participation are large and should not be minimized: inexperience, untested capacity, a transitory status which means that present action does not carry with it subsequent responsibility, and the inescapable fact that the other components of the institution are in a position of judgment over the students. It is important to recognize that student needs are strongly related to educational experience, both formal and informal. Students expect, and have a right to expect, that the educational process will be structured, that they will be stimulated by it to become independent adults, and that they will have effectively transmitted to them the cultural heritage of the larger society. If institutional support is to have its fullest possible meaning it should incorporate the strength, freshness of view, and idealism of the student body.

The respect of students for their college or university can be enhanced if they are given at least these opportunities: (1) to be listened to in the classroom without fear of institutional reprisal for the substance of their views, (2) freedom to discuss questions of institutional policy and operation, (3) the right to academic due process when charged with serious violations of institutional regulations, and (4) the same right to hear speakers of their own choice as is enjoyed by other components of the institution.

Student Participation in College and University Government: A Report of Committee T, 1970

INTRODUCTION The purpose of this report is to define the principles and identify several appropriate areas of student participation in the
government of colleges and universities. The report itself is
based on the premise that students as members of the academic
community, in addition to their rights as set forth in the *Joint
Statement on Rights and Freedoms of Students,* have a distinctive
role which, in respects stated below, qualifies them to share in
the exercise of responsible authority on campus; the exercise of
that authority is part of their education. Furthermore, there is a
greater likelihood of responsible student involvement when
students participate in institutional decisions through orderly
processes and to the degree appropriate in particular circumstances.

Most importantly, joint effort among all groups in the institution—students, faculty, administration, and governing
board—is a prerequisite of sound academic government. A further prerequisite is that all must see themselves as custodians of
academic freedom. Like any other group, students should have
a voice, sometimes the predominant voice, in decisions which
affect them, and their opinions should be regularly solicited

NOTE: [The 1966 Statement of Government of Colleges and Universities was]
jointly formulated by the American Association of University Professors, the
American Council on Education, and the Association of Governing Boards of
Universities and Colleges. The AAUP Council adopted the Statement in 1966,
and the Fifty-third Annual Meeting in April, 1967; the ACE and AGB have
commended it to their member institutions and boards. [It refers to students as
"an institutional component coordinate in importance with trustees, administrators, and faculty," notes that "students do not in fact presently have a significant voice in the government of colleges and universities," and expresses the
hope that the educational community will "turn its attention to an important
need."]

Other statements deal with the protections due the individual student or faculty member: the 1940 *Statement of Principles on Academic Freedom and Tenure;*
the 1958 *Statement on Procedural Standards in Faculty Dismissal Proceedings* (the
basic policy statements, formulated and adopted by the American Association
of University Professors and the Association of American Colleges, relating to
academic freedom, tenure, and academic due process); the 1967 *Joint Statement
of Rights and Freedoms of Students,* approved by the American Association of
University Professors, U.S. National Student Personnel Administrators, and
National Association of Women Deans and Counselors; and the 1971 *Procedure
Standards in the Renewal or Nonrenewal of Faculty Appointments.*

SOURCE: Reprinted from *AAUP Policy Documents and Reports,* 1973 Edition.

even in those areas in which they hold a secondary interest. But academic government depends on more than the accommodation of diverse interests. Joint effort, to be effective, must be rooted in the concept of shared authority. The exercise of shared authority in college and university government, like the protection of academic freedom, requires tolerance, respect, and a sense of community which arises from participation in a common enterprise. The exact mode and extent of student participation depend on conditions which vary from one institution to another; but whatever the area of participation or the form it assumes, the need for cooperation among all groups is inescapable.

STUDENT PARTICIPATION IN ACADEMIC AFFAIRS The rights of students to free inquiry and expression in the classroom and in conference is asserted in the *Joint Statement on Rights and Freedoms of Students*. Students also have a stake in the quality of their formal education, which must take into account their needs and desires. The categories which follow are those in which student involvement is commonly found; they are not intended to exclude other areas of involvement, which might be developed where there is sufficient student interest. It is for the particular institution to determine the mode and extent of student involvement and the criteria of eligibility for that involvement.

Admissions Students have a stake in the size, composition, and quality of the student body, and should have their views on admissions heard along with those of faculty and administration. Similarly, graduate students should be able to participate constructively in decisions regarding the admissions policy of their respective departments.

Academic programs Students should be consulted in decisions regarding the development of already-existing programs and the establishment of new programs. As members of the academic community they should have the opportunity for similar involvement with respect to course load and degree requirements. For example, they may submit reports to the administration or the appropriate faculty or departmental committees through their own curriculum committees, or through membership in joint curriculum committees. When provision is made for an experimental student-operated curriculum, students should have primary responsibility for decision-making.[1] When provision is made for student participation in curricular decisions, criteria for eligibility should be devised jointly by faculty and students.

Academic courses and staff Students should have the opportunity, through established institutional mechanisms, to assess the value of a course to them, and to make suggestions as to its direction. Students should also be able to express their views on the form and conduct of a class which they have taken, for example through an evaluative questionnaire prepared by joint faculty-student effort, and their opinions should be weighed in faculty decisions affecting faculty status. The faculty member, of course, should be duly protected from capricious and uninformed judgment by students, just as he should be from such judgment by anyone else.

Academic evaluation The method by which students are evaluated is properly of concern to them. Accordingly, students should be heard with respect to the grading system at an institution. They should also have clearly established means of recourse against prejudiced or capricious grading.

Academic environment The scheduling of courses, class size, distribution of night and day classes, calendar arrangements, library policy and development, and similar academic arrangements and services affect the ability of students to do academic work. They should share in the formation of policies on these matters.

STUDENT PARTICIPATION IN OTHER INSTITUTIONAL AFFAIRS *Extracurricular activities* Students should have primary responsibility for activities sponsored by the student body. Other appropriate persons and groups should be able to discuss such activities and be consulted with respect to them. Among these activities are cultural programs sponsored by the student body, student political affairs, and student publications; the intellectual vitality and academic freedom of the student body will be

[1] By "primary responsibility" is meant the ability to take action which has the force of legislation and can be overruled only in rare instances and for compelling reasons stated in detail.

insured in such activities by adequate representation of student taste and opinion.

Student regulations Students should have primary responsibility for the formulation of clear and readily available regulations pertaining to their personal lives, subject only to such restrictions as may be imposed by law.

Student discipline Students should have the opportunity to participate in establishing standards and procedures which govern student discipline, and take part also in the actual disciplinary process. Disciplinary proceedings should be in accordance with the provisions of the *Joint Statement on Rights and Freedoms of Students.*

Other institutional concerns Students have a right to be heard, through formal means, on questions involving an institution's budget, its physical resources, and its relationship with groups or agencies external to the campus. Provisions should exist for the transmission of student views on such matters to the faculty, president, and governing board.

IMPLEMENTATION The implementation of the above principles is properly subject to innumerable local variations. On students themselves falls the difficult task of assuring that the diversity of student interests and opinions is adequately represented. All individuals and groups at an institution should support the development of appropriate forms of student participation by assuring that organizations purporting to represent student interests possess a mandate from a clearly defined electorate, are accountable to that electorate, and function through orderly procedures agreed upon through joint action by students and the other members of the academic community. Student representatives, like other representatives in any area of university government, should be free to vote according to their best judgment. At all times, students should enjoy protection from the exercise of tyranny by a majority or a minority, the right to petition for and be granted an open hearing on a question of student rights or student participation, and the right of access—both to information on institutional government and to grievance procedures for complaints relating to their life in and out of the classroom.

Limits on participation by students may be dictated in some instances, such as those in which a violation of law or of confidentiality might result. Where any limitation exists, the student should have the right to challenge it in a manner consistent with legality and the principles of academic freedom. All forms of participation in the government of the institution should be so devised as to preserve the academic freedom to which all groups are equally entitled.

Student involvement in institutional government may include membership—voting and nonvoting—on departmental committees, on college or division councils and committees, or on the university senate or any other principal legislative body and its committees. Where they do not hold membership on these bodies, students should be able to place matters for action on their agendas and to receive a prompt report on the disposition of those matters. Student opinion should also be consulted, where feasible, in the selection of presidents, chief academic and nonacademic administrative officers including the dean of students, and faculty. Sometimes separate and parallel student structures are desired in place of or in addition to mixed bodies. Where this is the case, care should be taken to guarantee that the student bodies not function merely as subordinate entities subject to arbitrary veto by faculty or administrative groups, and that all groups enjoy meaningful channels of appeal. The procedure for election or appointment of students to duly constituted instruments of student participation should be developed in consultation with all directly concerned persons and groups. It should be made available as information to the entire campus community, and be reviewed periodically.

Meaningful participation in college and university government is not guaranteed merely by the presence of students on committees; in some cases, indeed, this may inhibit free student expression. Such expression may well play an important role in institutional affairs through the campus newspaper, published evaluations of courses, or discussion programs on the state of the institution which bring different constituencies together. In any case, the informal exchange of opinion, like the formal participation in the processes of institutional government, should involve students, faculty, administration, and governing board in a continuing joint effort.

**Faculty Participation in the Selection and Retention of Administrators:
A Report by Committee T, 1972**

INTRODUCTION   The 1966 *Statement on Government of Colleges and Universities* rests largely upon the conviction that interdependence, communication, and joint action among the constituents of a college or university enhance the institution's ability to solve educational problems. As one facet of this interdependence, the *Statement* asserts the expectation that faculty members will have a significant role in the selection of academic administrators, including the president, academic deans, department heads, and chairmen.[1] As a corollary, it is equally important that faculty members contribute significantly to judgments and decisions regarding the retention or nonretention of the administrators whom they have helped select.

THE SELECTION
OF
ADMINISTRATORS   The *Statement* emphasizes the primary role of faculty and board in the search for a president. The search may be initiated either by separate committees of the faculty and board or by a joint committee of the faculty and board or of faculty, board,

---

[1] According to the *Statement* ("Statement on Government of Colleges and Universities," *AAUP Bulletin*, LII [Winter, 1966], pp. 375–9):

"Joint effort of a most critical kind must be taken when an institution chooses a new president. The selection of a chief administrative officer should follow upon cooperative search by the governing board and the faculty, taking into consideration the opinions of others who are appropriately interested. The president should be equally qualified to serve both as the executive officer of the governing board and as the chief academic officer of the institution and the faculty. His dual role requires that he be able to interpret to board and faculty the educational views and concepts of institutional government of the other. He should have the confidence of the board and the faculty.

"The selection of academic deans and other chief academic officers should be the responsibility of the president with the advice of and in consultation with the appropriate faculty." (p. 377)

"The chairman or head of a department, who serves as the chief representative of his department within an institution, should be selected either by departmental election or by appointment following consultation with members of the department and of related departments; appointments should normally be in conformity with department members' judgment. The chairman or department head should not have tenure in his office; his tenure as a faculty member is a matter of separate right. He should serve for a stated term but without prejudice to re-election or to reappointment by procedures which involve appropriate faculty consultation." (p. 378)

SOURCE: Reprinted from *AAUP Bulletin*, Summer Issue, June 1972.

students, and others; and separate committees may subsequently be joined. In a joint committee, the numbers from each constituency should reflect both the primacy of faculty concern and the range of other groups, including students, that have a legitimate claim to some involvement. Each major group should elect its own members to serve on the committee, and the rules governing the search should be arrived at jointly. A joint committee should determine the size of the majority which will be controlling in making an appointment. When separate committees are used, the board, with whom the legal power of appointment rests, should either select a name from among those submitted by the faculty committee or should agree that no person will be chosen over the objections of the faculty committee.

The *Statement on Government* indicates that the faculty role is not as fully coordinate with the selection of academic deans and other administrative officers as it is with respect to the selection of a president. Some academic administrators whose role is almost entirely that of advisor to the president are less directly accountable to the faculty than is the president himself, and they must, therefore, be congenial or at least acceptable to him. Other academic administrators, such as the academic dean, or the dean of a college or other academic subdivision, are by the nature of their duties more directly dependent on faculty support. In such instances, a primary faculty role in the search is highly desirable, and may be particularly critical in institutions where the dean plays a directly influential role *vis-à-vis* the faculty. Even here, however, the president, after fully weighing the views of the faculty, must make the final choice. Nonetheless, sound academic practice dictates that he not choose a person over the reasoned opposition of the faculty.

THE RETENTION OF ADMINISTRATORS The decision to retain or, more significantly, not to retain an administrator should be subject to the same deliberative process and made by the same groups responsible for his selection. Whereas the *selection* of an administrator is essentially an exercise in foresight, a decision respecting his retention affords the opportunity for relevant academic groups to assess, on the basis of experience, the confidence in which the administrator is held.

The faculty role in determining the retention of academic deans and others at this administrative level should be co-extensive with the faculty role in their selection. Just as sound academic practice suggests that the president not choose an administrator seriously objectionable to the faculty, sound practice also dictates that he neither retain the administrator found wanting by faculty standards, nor that he arbitrarily dismiss an administrator who meets the accountability standards of the academic community. In either case his final judgment should be made subject to consultation with the administrator's relevant constituency and preferably by an institutionalized and jointly determined procedure.

With respect to the chief administrative officer, the 1966 *Statement* specifies that the "leadership role" of the president "is supported by delegated authority from the board and faculty." His retention of authority, therefore, like his acquisition of it, should be subject to the confidence in which he is held by faculty and board. Rather than assuming that he has acquired *de facto* tenure in his position as president, some system should be sought which would reflect from time to time the level of confidence he enjoys.

Such a system might take the form of a term appointment, near the end of which the president's term could be reviewed by formal or informal agreement, and he could be reappointed for another term or not be reappointed. Alternatively, at the request of either the board or the faculty, a joint review of his status might be made.

In any event, principal administrative officers should not be dismissed for any reason without significant involvement of the faculty of an institution. They should be protected from arbitrary removal by evolving procedures through joint effort, by which both their rights and the interests of various constituencies are adequately safeguarded.

Statement on Collective Bargaining, 1972

Collective bargaining, in offering a rational and equitable means of distributing resources and of providing recourse for an aggrieved individual, can buttress and complement the sound principles and practices of higher education which the American Association of University Professors has long supported. Where appropriate, therefore, the Association will pursue collective bargaining as a major additional way of realizing its goals in higher education, and it will provide assistance on a selective basis to interested local chapters.[1]

As large segments of the American faculty community manifest an interest in collective bargaining, there is a pressing need to develop a specialized model of collective bargaining in keeping with the standards of higher education. From its vantage point as the paramount national organization in formulating and implementing the principles that govern relationships of academic life, the Association has the unique potential, indeed the responsibility, to achieve through its chapters a mode of collective bargaining consistent with the best features of higher education. To leave the shaping of collective bargaining to organizations lacking the established dedication to principles developed by the Association and widely accepted by the academic community endangers those principles. To the extent that the Association is influential in the shaping of collective bargaining, the principles of academic freedom and tenure and the primary responsibility of a faculty for determining academic policy will be secured.

The longstanding programs of the Association are means to achieve a number of basic ends at colleges and universities: the enhancement of academic freedom and tenure; of due process; of sound academic government. Collective bargaining, properly used, is essentially another means to achieve these ends, and at the same time to strengthen the influence of the faculty in the distribution of an institution's economic resources. The implementation of Association-supported principles, reliant upon professional traditions and upon moral suasion, can be effec-

---

[1] Operating procedures for assisting chapters interested in collective bargaining are available from the Association's Washington Office.

SOURCE: Reprinted from *AAUP Bulletin*, Winter Issue, December 1972.

tively supplemented by a collective bargaining agreement and given the force of law.

When a chapter of the Association attains the status of representative of the faculty, it will seek to:

1 Protect and promote the economic and professional interests of the faculty as a whole in accordance with the established principles of the Association.

2 Establish within the institution democratic structures which provide full participation by all faculty members in accordance with the *Statement on Government of Colleges and Universities.*

3 Obtain explicit guarantees of academic freedom and tenure in accordance with the 1940 *Statement of Principles on Academic Freedom and Tenure,* the 1958 *Statement on Procedural Standards in Faculty Dismissal Proceedings,* the 1971 *Statement on Procedural Standards in the Renewal or Nonrenewal of Faculty Appointments,* and other policy statements of the Association.

4 Create an orderly and clearly defined procedure within the faculty governmental structure for prompt consideration of problems and grievances of faculty members, to which procedure any affected individual or group shall have full access.

In any agency shop or compulsory dues check-off arrangement, a chapter or other Association agency should incorporate provisions designed to accommodate affirmatively asserted conscientious objection to such an arrangement with any representative.

It is the policy of the Association (with which chapters should comply whether or not they are acting in a representative capacity) to call or support a faculty strike or other work stoppage only in extraordinary situations which so flagrantly violate academic freedom or the principles of academic government, or which are so resistant to rational methods of discussion, persuasion, and conciliation, that faculty members may feel impelled to express their condemnation by withholding their services, either individually or in concert with others. It should be assumed that faculty members will exercise their right to strike only if they believe that another component of the institution (or a controlling agency of government, such as a legislature or governor) is inflexibly bent on a course which undermines an essential element of the educational process. (See the Association's provisional *Statement on Faculty Participation in Strikes*).

Statement on Procedural Standards in the Renewal or Nonrenewal of Faculty Appointments, 1971

INTRODUCTION The steady growth in the number of institutions new to college and university traditions, and in the number of probationary faculty members, has underscored the need for adequate procedures in reaching decisions on faculty renewals and for the protection of the probationary faculty member against decisions either in violation of his academic freedom or otherwise improper.[1] Related to this need has been a heightened interest in providing the faculty member with a written statement of reasons for a decision not to offer him reappointment or to grant him tenure. At the Association's Fifty-fifth Annual Meeting, held on April 30 and May 1, 1969, a motion was adopted urging Committee A

. . . to consider adoption of the position that notice of nonreappointment of probationary faculty be given in writing and that it include the reasons for the termination of the appointment. In any allegation that the reasons are false, or unsupported by the facts, or violative of academic freedom or procedures, the proof should rest with the faculty member.

The position which the Annual Meeting urged Committee A to consider had been the primary topic of discussion at the December 14-15, 1968, meeting of the Committee A Subcommittee on Nontenured Faculty, and it was discussed at length again at the subcommittee's meeting on October 11, 1969, at the regular Committee A meetings of April 27–28 and October 29–30, and at a special meeting of Committee A on January 9–10, 1970. The present statement embodies the consensus arrived at during those meetings.

It has long been the Association's position, as stated in *The Standards for Notice of Nonreappointment*, that "notice of nonreappointment, or of intention not to recommend reappointment to the governing board, should be given in writing." Although the Association has not attempted to discourage the giving of reasons, either orally or in writing, for a notice of nonreappointment, it has not required that reasons be given.

---

[1] These procedures do not apply to special appointments, clearly designated in writing at the outset as involving only a brief association with the institution for a fixed period of time.

SOURCE: Reprinted from *AAUP Bulletin*, Summer Issue, June 1971.

In considering this question, Committee A endeavored to appraise the advantages and disadvantages of the Association's present policy and the proposed policy in terms of the Association's traditional concern for the welfare of higher education and its various components, including probationary faculty members. The committee also examined the question of giving reasons in the context of the entire probationary period. As a result, this statement goes beyond the question of giving reasons to the more fundamental subject of general fairness in the procedures related to renewal or nonrenewal of term appointments and the granting of tenure.

Statement

THE PROBATIONARY PERIOD: STANDARDS AND CRITERIA The 1940 *Statement of Principles on Academic Freedom and Tenure* prescribes that "during the probationary period a teacher should have the academic freedom that all other members of the faculty have." A number of the nontenured faculty member's rights provide support for his academic freedom. He cannot, for example, be dismissed before the end of a term appointment except for adequate cause which has been demonstrated through academic due process—a right he shares with tenured members of the faculty. If he asserts that he has been given notice of nonreappointment in violation of academic freedom, he is entitled to an opportunity to establish his claim in accordance with Section 10 of Committee A's *Recommended Institutional Regulations.* He is entitled to timely notice of nonreappointment in accordance with the schedule prescribed in the statement on *The Standards for Notice of Nonreappointment.*[2]

[2] The *Standards for Notice* are as follows:
(1) *Not later than March 1 of the first academic year of service,* if the appointment expires at the end of that year; or, if a one-year appointment terminates during an academic year, at least three months in advance of its termination.
(2) *Not later than December 15 of the second academic year of service,* if the appointment expires at the end of that year; or, if an initial two-year appointment terminates during an academic year, at least six months in advance of its termination.
(3) At least twelve months before the expiration of an appointment after two or more years in the institution.

Lacking the reinforcement of tenure, however, the academic freedom of the probationary faculty member has depended primarily upon the understanding and support of his faculty colleagues, the administration, and professional organizations, especially the Association. In the 1966 *Statement on Government of Colleges and Universities,* the Association and other sponsoring organizations have asserted that "faculty status and related matters are primarily a faculty responsibility; this area includes appointments, reappointments, decisions not to reappoint, promotions, the granting of tenure, and dismissal." It is Committee A's view that collegial deliberation of the kind envisioned by the *Statement on Government* will minimize the risk both of a violation of academic freedom and of a decision which is arbitrary or based upon inadequate consideration.

Frequently the young faculty member has had no training or experience in teaching, and his first major research endeavor may still be uncompleted at the time he starts his career as a college teacher. Under these circumstances, it is particularly important that there be a probationary period—a maximum of seven years under the 1940 *Statement of Principles on Academic Frredom and Tenure*—before tenure is granted. Such a period gives the individual time to prove himself, and his colleagues time to observe and evaluate him on the basis of his performance in the position rather than on the basis only of his education, training, and recommendations.

Good practice requires that the institution (department, college, or university) define its criteria for reappointment and tenure and its procedures for reaching decisions on these matters. The 1940 *Statement of Principles* prescribes that "the precise terms and conditions of every appointment should be stated in writing and be in the possession of both institution and teacher before the appointment is consummated." Committee A also believes that fairness to the faculty member prescribes that he be informed, early in his appointment, of the substantive and procedural standards which will be followed in determining whether or not his appointment will be renewed or tenure will be granted.

We accordingly make the following recommendation:

1. *Criteria and notice of standards* The faculty member should be advised, early in his appointment, of the substantive and

procedural standards generally employed in decisions affecting renewal and tenure. Any special standards adopted by his department or school should also be brought to his attention.

The relationship of the senior and junior faculty should be one of colleagueship, even though the nontenured faculty member knows that in time he will be judged by his senior colleagues. Thus the procedures adopted for evaluation and possible notification of nonrenewal should not endanger this relationship where it exists, and should encourage it where it does not. The nontenured faculty member should have available to him the advice and assistance of his senior colleagues; and the ability of senior colleagues to make a sound decision on renewal or tenure will be enhanced if an opportunity is provided for a regular review of the qualifications of nontenured faculty members. Total separation of the faculty roles in counseling and evaluation may not be possible and may at times be unproductive: for example, an evaluation, whether interim or at the time of final determination of renewal or tenure, can be presented in such a manner as to assist the nontenured faculty member as he strives to improve his performance.

Any recommendation regarding renewal or tenure should be reached by an appropriate faculty group in accordance with procedures approved by the faculty. Because it is important both to the faculty member and the decision-making body that all significant information be considered, he should be notified that a decision is to be made regarding renewal of his appointment or the granting of tenure and should be afforded an opportunity to submit material in writing which he believes to be relevant to that decision.

We accordingly make the following recommendations:

2(a) Periodic review There should be provision for periodic review of the faculty member's situation during the probationary service.

2(b) Opportunity to submit material The faculty member should be advised of the time when decisions affecting renewal and tenure are ordinarily made, and he should be given the opportunity to submit material which he believes will be helpful to an adequate consideration of his circumstances.

Observance of the practices and procedures outlined above should minimize the likelihood of reasonable complaint if the nontenured faculty member is given notice of nonreappointment. He will have been informed of the criteria and procedures for renewal and tenure; he will have been counseled by faculty colleagues; he will have been given an opportunity to have all material relevant to his evaluation considered; and he will have received a timely decision representing the view of faculty colleagues.

NOTICE OF REASONS With respect to giving reasons for a notice of nonreappointment, practice varies widely from institution to institution, and sometimes within institutions. At some, in accordance with the institution's regulations, the faculty member is provided with a written statement of the reasons. At others, generally at the discretion of the department chairman, he is notified of the reasons, either orally or in writing, if he requests such notification. At still others, no statement of reasons is provided even upon request, although information is frequently provided informally by faculty colleagues.

Resolving the question of whether a faculty member should be given a statement of reasons, at least if he requests it, requires an examination of the needs both of the institution and of the individual faculty member.

A major responsibility of the institution is to recruit and retain the best qualified faculty within its means. In a matter of such fundamental importance, the institution, through the appropriate faculty agencies, must be accorded the widest latitude consistent with academic freedom and the standards of fairness. Committee A recognizes that the requirement of giving reasons may lead, however erroneously, to an expectation that the decision-making body must justify its decision. A notice of nonreappointment may thus become confused with dismissal for cause, and under these circumstances the decision-making body may become reluctant to reach adverse decisions which may culminate in grievance procedures. As a result there is a risk that the important distinction between tenure and probation will be eroded.

To be weighed against these important institutional concerns are the interests of the individual faculty member. He may be honestly unaware of the reasons for a negative decision, and the decision may be based on a judgment of shortcomings which he could easily remedy if informed of them. A decision not to renew an appointment may be based on erroneous information which the faculty member could readily correct if he were informed of the basis for the decision. Again, the decision may be based on considerations of institutional policy or program development which have nothing to do with the faculty member's competence in his field, and if not informed of the reasons he may mistakenly assume that a judgment of inadequate performance on his part has been made. In the face of a persistent refusal to supply the reasons, a faculty member may be more inclined to attribute improper motivations to the decision-making body or to conclude that its evaluation has been based upon inadequate consideration. If he wishes to request a reconsideration of the decision, or a review by another body, his ignorance of the reasons for the decision will create difficulties both in reaching a decision whether to initiate such a request and in presenting his case for reconsideration or review.

After careful evaluation of these competing concerns, Committee A has concluded that the reasons in support of the faculty member's being informed outweigh the countervailing risks. Committee A emphasizes that in reaching this conclusion it does not consider it appropriate to require that every notice of nonreappointment be accompanied by a written statement of the reasons for nonreappointment. It may not always be to the advantage of the faculty member to be informed of the reasons, particularly in writing. If he is informed of them, he can be placed under an obligation to divulge them to the appointing body of another institution if it inquires why he is leaving his present position. Similarly, a written record is likely to become the basis for continuing responses by his former institution to prospective appointing bodies and may thus jeopardize his chances for obtaining positions over an extended period.

At many institutions, moreover, the procedures of evaluation and decision may make it difficult, if not impossible, to compile a statement of reasons which precisely reflects the basis of the decision. When a number of faculty members participate in the decision, they may oppose a reappointment for a variety of reasons, few or none of which may represent a majority view. To include every reason, no matter how few have held it, in a written statement to the faculty member may misrepresent the general view and damage unnecessarily both the faculty member's morale and his professional future.

In many situations, of course, a decision not to reappoint will not reflect adversely upon the faculty member. An institution may, for example, find it necessary for financial or other reasons to restrict its offerings in a given department. A number of institutions appoint more faculty members than they expect to give tenure; at such institutions a limit has been placed on the number of faculty at each rank, and the acquisition of tenure depends not only upon satisfactory performance but also upon an opening in the ranks above instructor or assistant professor. Nonrenewal in these cases is not likely to be psychologically damaging or to suggest a serious adverse judgment.

In these situations, providing a statement of reasons, either written or oral, should pose no difficulty, and such a statement may in fact assist the faculty member in his search for a new position. In other situations, in spite of his awareness of the considerations cited above, the faculty member may ask to be advised of the reasons which contributed to his nonreappointment, and Committee A believes that he should be given such advice. It believes also that he should have the opportunity to request a reconsideration by the decision-making body.

We accordingly make the following recommendation:

3. Notice of reasons In the event of a decision not to renew his appointment, the faculty member should be informed of the decision in writing, and, if he so requests, he should be advised of the reasons which contributed to that decision. He should also have the opportunity to request a reconsideration by the decision-making body.

WRITTEN REASONS Having been given orally the reasons which contributed to his nonreappointment, the faculty member, to avoid misunderstanding, may request that they be confirmed in writing. He may wish to petition the appropriate faculty committee, in accordance with Section 10 of Committee A's *Recommended Institutional Regulations,* to consider an allegation that the reasons he was given violate his academic freedom, or that the primary reasons for the notice of nonreappointment were not stated and constitute a violation of his academic freedom. He may wish to petition a committee, in accordance with Section 15 of the *Rec-*

ommended Institutional Regulations, to consider a complaint that the decision resulted from inadequate consideration and was therefore unfair to him. He may feel that a written statement of reasons may be useful to him in pursuing his professional career.

If the department chairman or other appropriate institutional officer to whom the request is made feels that confirming the oral statement in writing may be damaging to the faculty member on grounds such as those cited earlier in this statement, Committee A believes that it would be desirable for him to explain the possible adverse consequences of confirming the oral statement in writing. If in spite of this explanation the faculty member continues to request a written statement, Committee A believes that his request should be honored.

We accordingly make the following recommendation:

4. *Written reasons* If the faculty member expresses a desire to petition the grievance committee (such as is described in Sections 10 and 15 of Committee A's *Recommended Institutional Regulations*), or any other appropriate committee, to use its good offices of inquiry, recommendation, and report, or if he makes the request for any other reason satisfactory to himself alone, he should have the reasons given in explanation of the nonrenewal confirmed in writing.

REVIEW PROCEDURES: ALLEGATIONS OF ACADEMIC FREEDOM VIOLATIONS The best safeguard against a proliferation of grievance petitions on a given campus is the observance of sound principles and procedures of academic freedom and tenure and of institutional government. Committee A believes that observance of the procedures recommended in this statement—procedures which would provide guidance to nontenured faculty members, help assure them of a fair professional evaluation, and enlighten them concerning the reasons contributing to key decisions of their colleagues—would constitute a further step in the achievement of harmonious faculty relationships and the development of well-qualified faculties.

Even with the best practices and procedures, however, faculty members will at times feel that they have been improperly or unjustly treated and may wish another faculty group to review a decision of the faculty body immediately involved. Committee A believes that fairness both to the individual and the institution requires that the institution provide for such a review when it is requested. A possible violation of academic freedom is of vital concern to the institution as a whole, and where a violation is alleged it is of cardinal importance to the faculty and the administration to determine whether substantial grounds for the allegation exist. The institution should also be concerned to see that decisions respecting reappointment are based upon adequate consideration, and provision should thus be made for a review of allegations by affected faculty members that the consideration has been inadequate.

Because of the broader significance of a violation of academic freedom, Committee A believes that the procedures to be followed in these two kinds of complaints should be kept separate. Section 10 of the *Recommended Institutional Regulations*, mentioned earlier in this statement, provides a specific procedure for the review of complaints that academic freedom has been violated.[3]

If a faculty member on probationary or other nontenured appointment alleges that considerations violative of academic freedom significantly contributed to a decision not to reappoint him, his allegation will be given preliminary consideration by the [insert name of committee], which will seek to settle the matter by informal methods. His allegation shall be accompanied by a statement that he agrees to the presentation, for the consideration of the faculty committees, of such reasons and evidence as the institution may allege in support of its decision. If the difficulty is unresolved at this stage, and if the committee so recommends, the matter will be heard in the manner set forth in Regulations 5 and 6, except that the faculty member making the complaint is responsible for stating the grounds upon which he bases his allegations, and the burden of proof shall rest upon him. If he succeeds in establishing a *prima facie* case, it is incumbent upon those who made the decision not to reappoint him to come forward with evidence in support of their decision.

We accordingly make the following recommendation:

5. *Petition for review alleging an academic freedom violation* Insofar as the petition for review alleges a violation of academic

---

[3] Because the *Recommended Institutional Regulations* remain under review by Committee A, faculties processing complaints under Sections 10 and 15 may wish to secure the further advice of the Association's Washington Office.

freedom, the functions of the committee which reviews the faculty member's petition should be the following:

- To determine whether or not the notice of nonreappointment constitutes on its face a violation of academic freedom.
- To seek to settle the matter by informal methods.
- If the matter remains unresolved, to decide whether or not the evidence submitted in support of the petition warrants a recommendation that a formal proceeding be conducted in accordance with Sections 5 and 6 of the *Recommended Institutional Regulations,* with the burden of proof resting upon the complaining faculty member.

REVIEW PROCEDURES: ALLEGATIONS OF INADEQUATE CONSIDERATION Complaints of inadequate consideration are likely to relate to matters of professional judgment, where the department or departmental agency should have primary authority. For this reason, Committee A believes that the basic functions of the review committee should be to determine whether adequate consideration was given to the appropriate faculty body's decision and, if it determines otherwise, to request reconsideration by that body.

It is easier to state what the standard "adequate consideration" does not mean than to specify in detail what it does. It does not mean that the review committee should substitute its own judgment for that of members of the department on the merits of whether the candidate should be reappointed or given tenure. The conscientious judgment of the candidate's departmental colleagues must prevail if the invaluable tradition of departmental autonomy in professional judgments is to prevail. The term "adequate consideration" refers essentially to procedural rather than substantive issues: Was the decision conscientiously arrived at? Was all available evidence bearing on the relevant performance of the candidate sought out and considered? Was there adequate deliberation by the department over the import of the evidence in the light of the relevant standards? Were irrelevant and improper standards excluded from consideration? Was the decision a *bona fide* exercise of professional academic judgment? These are the kinds of questions suggested by the standard "adequate consideration."

If in applying this standard the review committee concludes that adequate consideration was not given, its appropriate response should be to recommend to the department that it assess the merits once again, this time remedying the inadequacies of its prior consideration.

An acceptable review procedure, representing one procedural system within which such judgments may be made, is outlined in Section 15 of the *Recommended Institutional Regulations*, as follows:

If a faculty member feels that he has cause for grievance in any matter other than dismissal proceedings—such matters as salaries, assignment of teaching duties, assignment of space or other facilities, and propriety of conduct—he may petition the elected faculty grievance committee [here name the committee] for redress. The petition shall set forth in detail the nature of the grievance and shall state against whom the grievance is directed. It shall contain any factual or other data which the petitioner deems pertinent to his case. The committee will have the right to decide whether or not the facts merit a detailed investigation. Submission of a petition will not automatically entail investigation or detailed consideration thereof. The committee may seek to bring about a settlement of the issue satisfactory to the parties. If in the opinion of the committee such a settlement is not possible or is not appropriate, the committee will report its findings and recommendations to the petitioner and to the appropriate administrative officer and faculty body [here identify], and the petitioner will, at his request, be provided an opportunity to present his case to them.

The grievance committee will consist of three [or some other number] members of the faculty who have tenure and who are elected at large. No department chairman or administrative officer shall serve on the committee.

We accordingly make the following recommendation:

6. Petition for review alleging inadequate consideration Insofar as the petition for review alleges inadequate consideration, the functions of the committee which reviews the faculty member's petition should be the following:

- To determine whether the decision of the appropriate faculty body was the result of adequate consideration in terms of the relevant standards of the institution, with the understanding that the review committee should not substitute its judgment on the merits for that of the faculty body.
- To request reconsideration by the faculty body when the committee believes that adequate consideration was not given to the faculty

member's qualifications. (In such instances, the committee should indicate the respects in which it believes the consideration may have been inadequate.)

- To provide copies of its report and recommendation to the faculty member, the faculty body, and the president or other appropriate administrative officer.

Appendix E: University of Cambridge: First Report on Participation by Junior Members in the Educational Business of the University

One of our terms of reference is "to discuss matters which are primarily the concern of the university . . . and which are of interest to senior and junior members alike." Prominent among these matters is the question of participation by junior members in the business of the university. We are considering this matter and we beg to present a first report, which deals with participation in educational business at the level of faculties[1] and departments. Later in the term we expect to report on arrangements which have been or are being made for participation by junior members in the activities of some non-academic boards and syndicates. After this we propose to review the functions, composition, and mode of election of the committee.

THE CASE FOR PARTICIPATION We begin by accepting the view in the joint statement of the Committee of Vice-Chancellors and Principals and the National Union of Students,[2] that, over educational matters, "we would regard it as essential that students' views should be properly taken into account." In Cambridge the supervision system provides a continuous "feedback" from pupil to teacher but by itself this is not enough because the information which supervisors receive is not always communicated to the faculty board or department which can act on it. Accordingly faculty boards

---

[1] Faculties in Cambridge generally cover a wider range of subjects than a department in an American university and a narrower range than a faculty in a continental university. Sometimes they are coterminous with the scope of an American department, *e.g.*, faculty of history. [Editor.]

[2] For the full text of this statement, see "Students and Universities in Great Britain II," *Minerva*, VII, 1–2 (Autumn–Winter, 1968–69), pp. 67–72.

SOURCE: Reprinted with permission from *Minerva*, Vol. VII, No. 3, Spring 1969, pp. 454–464.

and departments were asked to inform the committee about the arrangements already in existence in them for communication between senior and junior members over educational matters. We found that, in some faculties and departments communication is already good and both senior and junior members appear to be satisfied with it, or arrangements to improve it are being made. In others there is, in our view, room for improvement in the opportunities for "students' views to be properly taken into account." We realise that responsibility for agreeing upon arrangements, provided they lie within the statutes and ordinances, is a matter for individual departments or faculties. Our purpose is to propose some principles which these arrangements might follow.

The joint statement referred to above distinguishes two areas covered by university committees concerned with academic business: an area (including curricula, teaching methods, and the pattern of examinations) in which students could properly be involved; and an area (including individual admissions, appointments, promotions, and academic assessment) where decision-making should be reserved to senior members. We accept this distinction as a general basis for our recommendations, noting, however, the proviso in that statement that in the latter area students should "have opportunities to discuss the general principles involved in such decisions and have their views properly considered."

The fact that junior members come to the university to learn, and senior members are appointed to teach, carries the assumption that, over educational matters, junior members acknowledge some authority vested in senior members. Therefore we do not base our recommendations on the view that universities ought to be reorganised as models of a political democracy, conferring upon all members, senior and junior, an equal right to participate in decision-taking at all levels. But we do unanimously agree that comment and criticism of the way the university fulfills its purpose is a right of all members, and if this right is to be exercised effectively by junior members there ought to be formally established ways for them to become involved in decisions which affect their education.

We realise that a majority of junior members are not normally interested in the university's business and are content to get on with their studies and their own affairs. This is true of a majority of senior members, too, who are content to leave the day-to-day management of the university in the hands of a few of their colleagues who are prepared to give time and trouble to committee work. It may well be that many junior members will not wish to avail themselves of opportunities for consultation or involvement. But this, in our view, is no reason for denying the opportunities to those junior members who are genuinely concerned that the student point of view should be taken into account in the improvement of education in the university, and who are prepared to take the trouble to discover what this point of view is and to put it to senior members.

We begin by setting out four principles which we regard as essential to any effective exercise of student influence in academic decisions:

1 Junior members who become involved in aspects of the university's business must be given full opportunity to master the issues. This means that they must have access to the necessary papers on the same basis as senior members. It means also that they must be willing to spend the considerable amount of time needed to read the papers and to acquire the necessary background information.

2 Whatever form participation takes, it must include free-and-equal discussion between senior and junior members about the issues, so that each have a chance to influence the other. The eventual decisions or recommendations should be the result of such discussion.

3 If the machinery of participation requires representatives to be elected, then it should be in such a way that junior members, like senior members, act in their personal deliberative capacities, serving as representatives and not as delegates specifically mandated by the body which nominated them. Moreover junior members, like senior members, should not be allowed to send proxies to meetings, for this could destroy the continuity of service which is essential if a committee is to be effective. The question of confidentiality does not in practice appear to be a difficult one. On the one hand committees need to have access to information which it would be improper to make public, and premature disclosure of the way in which a committee's mind is working may prejudice its final recommendations. On the other

hand both senior and junior members should be free to sound opinion on matters under discussion. We do not believe that the question of confidentiality presents any obstacle to our recommendations, for experience of staff-student committees in other universities indicates that junior members find it no more difficult than senior members to observe the kind of discretion needed on a committee.

4   The fourth principle is that of accountability. The student representative must retain the confidence of those who elected him, without sacrificing his own independence of judgement. This requires an effective means of communication, in both directions, between committees which include student representatives and the student electorate.

We believe that arrangements can be made for students to participate in the making of educational policy in ways consistent with these four principles. We now suggest ways in which this might be done.

Patterns of participation

If student representatives are to have an effective influence on educational planning they must be involved at the level where policies are worked out and determined. Ideas which affect teaching, curricula, and examinations originate "on the shop floor," *i.e.*, in departments and faculties. For any important educational change a committee makes recommendations which have to be scrutinised by faculty boards and the general board to ensure that they do not adversely affect the interests of other departments and faculties and that they do not involve expenditure which cannot be afforded. But the principle is that ideas flow "upwards" as recommendations to be approved, not "downwards" as directives to be obeyed. Therefore the crucial points for student participation are at the level of departments or faculties.

At this level there are several means whereby junior members may be enabled to participate in the formulation of educational policy and the management of academic affairs. All of them are being tried in various faculties and departments of the university. None of them is incompatible with the others, but because faculties and departments vary so much in size and nature, methods which are appropriate in one faculty or department may not be appropriate in others. It must, therefore, be for each faculty or department, in consultation with the students taught in the faculty or department, to decide how best to involve students in the management and formulation of educational policy. The following arrangements are suggested as possible means for so increasing student participation.

Informal arrangements The committee appreciate that in some faculties and departments, especially the smaller ones, the existing informal channels of communication have worked well and that neither senior nor junior members are dissatisifed with them. The committee would not wish to propose the introduction of more formal arrangements for consultation if there were a danger that this would damage the present informal relations but they think that in all departments, however small, there are good reasons for considering the adoption of a more formal system. Even if informal arrangements have hitherto proved adequate, it would be unwise to assume that a serious need for more formal arrangements will never arise. Experience elsewhere has led the committee to think that it is better to establish formal arrangements for consultation while relations between students and staff are good, than to defer agreement on formal procedures until they are most needed. A very difficult situation could arise if informal arrangements broke down and there were no agreed channels of communication.

Moreover, we believe that the establishment of some formal means of communication could encourage the crystallisation and detailed examination of ideas that arise through informal contact. Also, we think it desirable that in those faculties and departments which at present rely entirely on informal communication, students should have the assurance that their views will be given formal consideration.

Open meetings Notwithstanding specific arrangements which faculties and departments may make for representatives of senior and junior members to deal with educational matters, we think it desirable that there should also be regular meetings, at least once a year, open to all senior and junior members in a faculty (or department, depending on the faculty's organisation), where there can be an exchange of views, but no binding decisions taken, on matters of common interest.

Questionnaires Several departments have told us that they use questionnaires to discover student views on curricula and examinations and to give students an opportunity to comment anonymously on the courses given by individual teaching officers. They have said that they find the replies to such questionnaires valuable and constructive, often leading to reform of the curricula and examinations. We have noticed that, for the most part, it is the scientific departments which make use of questionnaires but we believe this method of ascertaining student views could be used to good effect by many other faculties and departments. We think that questionnaires are particularly valuable as an adjunct to more formal methods, in that they give all students concerned an opportunity to express their views whereas with either joint committees or presence at faculty boards only a representative minority can be involved.

Staff-student committees[3] The educational unit which makes decisions affecting a student's academic career is sometimes the department, sometimes the faculty. Except in departments or faculties where the senior and junior members agree that any formal means of student participation would be undesirable, the committee believe that some formal arrangements for regular consultation should be established where they do not already exist. One pattern is to have officially recognised staff-student committees attached either to departments or to faculty boards, whichever is the more appropriate unit. Where the faculty is subdivided into departments, and where there now exist education committees in such departments, these committees could be reconstituted as staff-student committees. Staff-student committees should consist of about equal numbers of senior and junior members, all having voting rights. They should consider all educational matters of interest to students, *e.g.*, teaching methods, curricula and courses, and patterns of examinations. Student involvement should not extend to such reserved items as personal appointments, promotions, and other matters relating to individual senior or junior members. Staff-student committees would have two main functions: (1) to

---

[3] We are not committed to this name for these committees. Possible alternatives are joint education committees, or faculty (or departmental) consultative committees.

act as points of origin for discussion about innovation and change in educational matters relating to the relevant faculty board or department, and (2) to discuss and comment on proposals formulated by the faculty board and affecting students, before such proposals reach the stage of decision. We should also expect, where appropriate, that faculty boards, instead of setting up *ad hoc* committees to consider specific educational problems, would ask the staff-student committee to undertake such commissions, or to nominate representatives of junior members to serve on such committees. The reports and recommendations of the staff-student committee would be made known to the faculty or department as a whole. All members of a faculty staff-student committee should attend faculty board meetings when their reports are discussed, and should have the right to speak.

The method of election of junior members to serve on staff-student committees may present problems because the electorates will not always be easy to define. It is for faculties and departments in the first instance to work out electoral systems to their own satisfaction. We make some general observations on this matter in an appendix.

Where staff-student committees are established we should regard as essential to their success that there should be adequate arrangements for two-way communication between the committees and all the junior members concerned. Access to the committee by junior members should be easy and they should be encouraged to make use of it. A junior member who wished to put ideas forward could well be asked to make a written submission, followed, unless the committee decided otherwise, by attendance at the committee to discuss his submission. This would encourage contributions by reasoned argument to the committee's work. At the same time junior members should be kept informed of the committee's activities, by the publication, on notice boards or in some other way, of its agenda, minutes, and reports and, so far is practicable, the reasons for its decisions.

Once a year each staff-student committee should make a report to the joint consultative committee on the working of its arrangements. After an experimental period consideration should be given by the general board, after consulting faculty boards and departments, to the desirability of providing enabling ordinances for staff-student committees, defining their powers, terms of reference, composition, and mode of election of both senior and junior members.

Faculty boards We would expect the staff-student committees, with the responsibilities which we propose [above], to be the bodies where educational problems of concern to students are worked out and formulated as proposals. But another experiment which we would ask faculty boards to consider, in addition to the establishment of staff-student committees, is the possibility of inviting junior members to attend faculty board meetings as observers, with full rights to speak but without voting rights. The exact number of junior members would of course be decided by each faculty board, but we believe that the purpose of doing this, where it is done, should not be merely to offer a token which would be little more than symbolic: it should be to enable junior members to make an effective contribution to the board's business. The observers should include graduates as well as undergraduates. The ratio between these two classes would be a matter for faculty boards to decide for themselves. The observers would not attend degree committees, nor would they be involved in the reserved items; and there would have to be a prior agreement on the exact area in which these reserved items fall.[4] Observers would be elected by junior members in ways acceptable to faculty boards; their participation would need to be consistent with the four principles set out [above].

The belief that the presence of junior members at meetings of faculty boards will make a positive contribution to the working of staff-student committees rests on the fact that, if junior members are to put forward realistic and useful ideas, they must understand what is feasible, and what is not, in educational change. It is arguable that the simplest way to acquire this understanding is to be present at meetings of faculty boards, where all relevant considerations are brought together for assessment.

---

[4] This area was described in the Joint Statement of the Vice-Chancellors' Committee and the National Union of Students as follows: "that involving, for example, decisions on appointments, promotions, and other matters affecting the personal position of members of staff, the admissions of individuals and their academic assessment."

There is no doubt that much of the misunderstanding and mistrust which arises from time to time between staff and students in universities throughout the country is simply due on one side to ignorance of how business is conducted, and, on the other side, to a misconception of the motives behind the proposals (often badly expressed due to that ignorance) which come from students who want changes in the pattern of their education. We believe that the presence of observers on faculty boards might diminish the risks of such misunderstanding, and that on this ground alone the experiment deserves serious consideration. We are the more convinced of this from our own experience on the consultative committee. It could be argued that mutual confidence between representatives of senior and junior members would not be assured if junior members attended faculty board meetings only for the discussion of their own particular proposals; and that the proper remedy is the greater familiarity between junior and senior members that would come from their sitting together at the faculty board.

Student presence at meetings of faculty boards might make the meetings longer, but it is arguable that this should be accepted as a natural consequence if student participation is to be taken seriously. And although the contribution of student observers to the business would inevitably be limited in some respects, their presence might well serve to disclose and represent an interest in matters which senior members might assume were routine and devoid of policy content.

The doubt about the value of student presence is based on the knowledge of how faculty boards actually work. They meet infrequently (six or eight times a year, not exclusively in term-time). Much of their business falls in the reserved area and a good deal of the remainder has to do with matters, such as grants for research projects, which are likely to be of marginal concern to junior members. Many items will inevitably require a continuity of membership and a long-range view of academic policy that must limit the possible contribution of junior members. Moreover, only occasionally, *e.g.,* in periods of Tripos[5] revision, do faculty boards engage in radical discussion of such matters as the curriculum, teaching methods, and examinations, and when such discussion is initiated it is almost in-

---

[5] Revision of syllabus or course of study. [Editor.]

variably first referred to a committee, since the normal business of the board would be disrupted by undigested discussion. In future these matters would presumably be referred to the staff-student committee, or it would be invited to join in setting up a specialist committee.

If student participation is to be effective it will be necessary for senior members to ensure that junior members can formulate their ideas against a proper background of information about the faculty's mode of operation and range of business. We would expect this background to be supplied at staff-student committees of the kind proposed, and it is arguable that presence on faculty boards, where miscellaneous business is done "against the clock", would, in this respect, offer no additional advantage. Confidence between the participants is essential for an effective exchange of ideas, and this may require some time to establish. But it is not certain that the way to establish it is through the presence of a few junior members for a part of the business of a limited number of faculty board meetings; indeed it is arguable that this might reduce the efficiency of the board without securing the kind of atmosphere which is essential for successful student participation.

In short, there are potential benefits in the suggestion that student observers should be invited to faculty board meetings; and there are doubts and objections. We believe that the potential benefits would justify experiments on these lines, and it is in this spirit that we unanimously commend the suggestion to the consideration of faculty boards.

Conclusion and recommendations

The pattern of participation by junior members in academic business is a matter of the greatest importance for the future relations between senior and junior members and for the welfare of the university as a whole. We believe that there must be some changes in this pattern, but that none of the changes should be imposed from above and all of them should be experimental; we also believe that the effect of any change must be to strengthen, not to weaken, the university as a place of learning and research. With these considerations in mind we unanimously make five recommendations, none of which requires any amendment to statute or ordinance. They are:

1   That where this has not already been done, staff-student committees, consistent with the four principles set out [above] should be set up, attached either to departments or to faculty boards. The choice must depend on the structure and inclinations of departments and faculties, but the arrangements must be comprehensive so that every student will know that there is a committee, at either the faculty or departmental level, to which he can make representations on academic matters.

2   That faculty boards should consider inviting student observers to attend faculty board meetings on the lines suggested [above].

3   That all arrangements, both for staff-student committees and for observers on any faculty boards which decide to invite them, should be regarded as experimental; and that the general board and the consultative committee should begin in the Lent Term 1970 to consider reports on such experience as may by then have been gained from the experiments.

4   That the suggestion . . . for open meetings at least once a year, where there can be an exchange of views but no binding decisions taken, should be commended to faculties (or departments, depending on the faculty's composition) which do not already arrange such meetings.

5   That the use of questionnaires to discover student views on curricula and examinations, on the lines suggested [above] should be commended to those faculties and departments which do not use them already.

Eric Ashby, Chairman	Ruth G. Loewenthal
I. M. Baker	R. E. Macpherson
L. Gibson	George Moore
C. B. Goodhart	S. L. Pemberton
David Harrison	F. D. Robinson
D. M. Joslin	T. J. Smiley
G. T. Kanfer	Jon Stern
V. W. Lee	P. Swinnerton-Dyer

APPENDIX 1   The constitution of joint faculty and departmental committees, and the election of junior members to attend meetings of faculty

boards, would present problems as regards both definition of the electorate and the method of voting. There is doubtless no ideal scheme and we do not imagine that any which we could propose would seem satisfactory in all circumstances. We therefore think it better to attempt no more than to identify the problems, suggest basic principles which it is desirable that any scheme should satisfy, and mention methods which we think faculties and departments may wish to consider. We think that, for an experimental period, faculties and departments should adopt whatever scheme seems best suited to their particular situation and we would only ask them to bear in mind that if, at a later stage, provision for such elections has to be made in the university ordinances, it will be essential that both the definition of the electorate and the method of voting should be capable of description in precise terms.

2   The difficulties which we foresee lie mainly in the election of representatives of the junior members. As regards senior members, faculty boards are accustomed to nominating representatives (not necessarily from their own number) to serve on other bodies and presumably would not wish to institute any formal machinery in respect of a faculty joint committee; they may, however, wish to consider whether the election of the senior members should be by the faculty as a whole, in the same manner, and at the same meeting, as the faculty elects members to represent it on the faculty board. As regards departmental committees, there is no statutory provision which could be used for this purpose. Presumably the head of a department could nominate the representatives of the senior members but we should think it preferable that nominations should be agreed at a departmental meeting of the teaching staff.

3   In devising methods for the election of representatives of junior members the following desiderata should be borne in mind:

- As high a proportion of the electorate as possible should take part in the election: this means that as far as possible the electors must have some means of knowing what the views of the candidates are on critical issues, and which of them are best qualified to put the student point of view in a persuasive and convincing way.

- Students at all stages of their studies, from freshmen to graduate students, must be represented: this is particularly important where, for example, very large numbers of undergraduates take Part I of a Tripos and much smaller numbers take Part II. Also, in most faculties and departments, graduate students will almost invariably be a minority but, as recent graduates, they would be particularly well qualified to contribute to the discussion of undergraduates' problems.

- As wide a range of student opinion as possible should be represented and there should therefore be some means of ensuring that minority groups are not excluded. . . .

4 If the elections were held on a faculty or departmental basis, the main alternative schemes appear to be as follows:

- The places to be filled would be divided into classes (*a*), (*b*), (*c*) and (*d*), representing first-, second-, third- and fourth-year undergraduates, and the graduate students. The number of places in each class might vary, *e.g.*, there might be two graduate students, three third-year undergraduates, two second-year undergraduates, and one freshman. The places might then be filled either (1) by the electorate voting only in the class in which they would themselves be qualified to be candidates, or (2) by the whole electorate voting on membership of each class.

- The students in a faculty or department might elect a committee to nominate representatives of the junior members on the joint committee and on any other sub-committee or working party which might be set up.

- In some departments and faculties there may already be well-established societies which could be asked to nominate junior members to the relevant joint committee. This method would, however, be likely to be acceptable only if the membership of the society were open to all junior members in the department or faculty and if the society did not include many members other than those who would be included in the electorate as defined above. . . .